WHEN THE
LITTLE THINGS
COUNT

...and They Always Count

BOOKS AUTHORED BY BARBARA PACHTER

The Power of Positive Confrontation

BOOKS CO-AUTHORED BY BARBARA PACHTER

The Prentice Hall Complete Business Etiquette Handbook

Business Etiquette

Minding Your Business Manners: Etiquette Tips for Presenting Yourself Professionally in Every Business Situation

Climbing the Corporate Ladder: What You Need to Know and Do to Be a Promotable Person

WHEN THE
LITTLE THINGS
COUNT

...and They Always Count

601 ESSENTIAL THINGS THAT
EVERYONE IN BUSINESS NEEDS TO KNOW

BARBARA PACHTER

WITH SUSAN MAGEE

Marlowe & Company
New York

Published by
Marlowe & Company
An Imprint of Avalon Publishing Group Incorporated
245 West 17th Street, 11th Floor
New York, NY 10011

WHEN THE LITTLE THINGS COUNT
... AND THEY ALWAYS COUNT
601 Essential Things that Everyone in Business Needs to Know

AVALON
publishing group incorporated

Copyright © 2001 by Barbara Pachter with Susan Magee

Library of Congress Cataloging-in-Publication Data

Pachter, Barbara.
When the little things count—and they always count / by
Barbara Pachter with Susan Magee.
p. cm.
ISBN 1-56924-625-4
1. Business etiquette. 2. Business communication. I. Magee, Susan. II. Title.

HF5389 .P3322001
650.1'3—dc21   00-048948

9   8   7   6   5   4

Designed by Serg Andreyev, Neuwirth & Associates, Inc.

Printed in the United States of America
Distributed by Publishers Group West

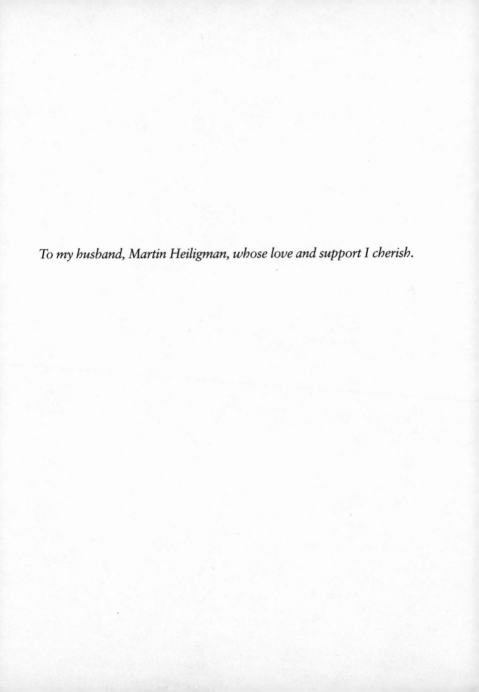

To my husband, Martin Heiligman, whose love and support I cherish.

CONTENTS

CONTENTS

WHEN THE LITTLE THINGS COUNT

...and They Always Count

INTRODUCTION

IN A PREVIOUS CAREER, I was a photographer for a major metropolitan newspaper. Though I ultimately chose to change careers and become a business communications trainer, a job I've now enjoyed for over twelve years, photography was challenging and great fun. I still love looking at good photographs.

I also believe that if I hadn't been a photographer, I would not be the corporate trainer that I am today. I certainly would not be writing this book. In fact, some of my best training for the seminars that I give I got from looking into the lens.

Photography taught me to "see." And it taught me that to see well enough to take excellent and memorable pictures I had to pay attention to the many "little things" that literally make up the bigger picture.

In photojournalism, the little things were made up of things like seeing the exact moment when the sun cast the perfect shadow, catching the wonderment in a man's eye as he saw his child for the first time, changing a woman's posture ever so slightly so the background no longer ruined the picture, or knowing the expression on the baseball player's face when he realizes he successfully stole home!

The skill to take a picture that tells a whole story or captures a fleeting moment or feeling may seem to have nothing to do with the little things say of techno-etiquette or how to write business memos effectively. But they do. The point is not what the specific dos and don'ts are. The point is understanding that sometimes it's the little things that make or break the photograph or the business meeting, the networking event, the e-mail memo, the presentation, the new client relationship and whether or not you're the one who leads the team, gets the promotion or the big bonus. You have to see the little things to shoot a good photograph and you have to learn to pay attention to the little things to present yourself professionally in today's business world.

And in business the little things always count—probably more than you know.

Why I Wrote this Book

I wrote this book for three reasons. One reason is that I want to help you understand that paying attention to the little things can help you get ahead—finally—and stay ahead—finally—in today's sometimes stormy, sometimes fascinating, sometimes satisfying, sometimes frustrating world of work.

Having met thousands of business people at all organizational levels—from the CEOs to the administrative assistants, I can tell you that people don't understand exactly how much the little things count in business until they ignore them and suffer the consequences—everything from embarrassment to reassignment and even job loss.

Meet:

- The Web master in a company who felt he needed to give unsolicited, negative feedback to others on their work even though they didn't work for him. He couldn't understand why he wasn't invited out with them on Friday nights.
- The American engineer who e-mailed her new German counterpart using first names after the man had e-mailed her using her last name. The American wondered why she got a cool reception when she received his answer. She didn't know that Germans approach business relationships very formally.
- The bank manager who swears he got his job because his boss got drunk at the holiday party and said offensive comments to others.
- The account manager who took his potential customers out to lunch and then proceeded to berate the waitress in front of them. He wondered why he didn't get the sale.
- The director of operations who answered his e-mails during a meeting. He was later reprimanded by his VP for not participating in the meeting.
- The pharmaceutical sales rep who leaned over and whispered to her customer during a business dinner, "I'm not wearing any underwear." She was overheard saying this and her co-workers no longer want her on their team.
- The customer service representative who told the customer he would call him back with the requested information about the product. He never did and lost the sale.

A Techno-Obsessed Business World

The second reason I'm writing this book has to do with a growing perception that in today's business world technology is everything!

Right?

Wrong.

Today there is indeed a strong preoccupation, even obsession, with the Internet, e-commerce, and the "new economy" that's been created. And rightly so! The Internet and all the new technology that's become a part of our daily lives has drastically changed the way we communicate and work—but only to a point. I believe that all of the hype about the new economy has a great number of people feeling like they're missing out and getting left behind. If only we too could get in on the ground floor of a new Internet venture then perhaps we too could buy our beachfront dream house (if not our own South Seas island!).

Well, let's all wake up from that dream, shake ourselves thoroughly to greet the new day and get on with the business of doing business. The reality is that most of us are not missing out and being left behind. Yes, there are opportunities to use the Internet and e-commerce to create new ventures and enhance the ways in which we do business. Some of those big opportunities were indeed big, but many went bust. The new e-economy is still in its early stages; it's still shaking itself out, revealing itself and evolving.

In the meantime, the reality is that most of us aren't doing enough with the opportunities we have every day to be more successful in the jobs we go to every day.

Truly smart business people understand that technological know-how, and computer and e-commerce skills will only get them so far on the path to long-term business success.

How do they get the rest of the way?

Yep. You guessed it—by paying attention to the little things that affect how others perceive you and how you perceive yourself. Little things that demonstrate that you can communicate and interact with others on a professional level regardless of your position or occupation. Little things that demonstrate you have what it takes to lead the discussion, the project or even the entire company.

Most of the 601 little things that count don't depend on having a secure server or the latest software. These are, for the most part, low-tech details like how to use e-mail appropriately, shake hands the right way, control your body language, use humor appropriately. These are relationship little things like knowing how to make others comfortable, navigate global business differences, network effectively, talk to others, eat in front of others, deal with difficult people. These are your employability essentials like how to be perceived as an expert, handle criticism, make decisions...the list goes on and on and on—all the way to 601 simple but very essential things that will help make you more successful, respected, and well-thought-of—right now.

If you think these kinds of little things can't derail even a techno-wonder's career, think again.

As I've said, I've been conducting business training for over twelve years to about as wide a variety of business professionals as you'll ever get. My clients include some of the world's leading business and e-commerce players, like NASA, Merck & Co., Nabisco and Ernst & Young. My clients are also small accounting firms, growing consulting companies and new dotcom start-ups. I have seen promising, even brilliant, careers derailed, side-tracked or blown sky high, simply because a person wasn't paying attention to the little things. Many business professionals are either ignorant of basic business etiquette skills and/or lacking essential communication skills, or worse, choose to ignore them.

It's almost hard to believe the mistakes, blunders and errors that business people make every day. These are otherwise smart, sometimes super smart, professionals.

Will these kinds of mistakes and blunders, even if made innocently, make the difference whether someone gets the raise, promotion, sale, or establishes the critical business relationship? Yes! I have seen it proven time and time again. I frequently hear these kinds of comments during my seminars: "Wow, I wish I had taken this seminar last month. This information would have helped with my customer" or "Oh, so that explains it..."

My third reason for writing this book is because the business professionals I work with every day have asked me for a quick-read guide packed with the absolutely essential skills they need to approach a variety of business situations and relationships with confidence and ease—whether it be a conference call with an Asian client, a high-pressure job interview over lunch, a company sales meeting or a confrontation with a co-worker.

This book is badly needed. The 601 essential things I talk about in these pages are rarely taught in college or business school. And given today's preoccupation with technology skills, it's even more critical. As I've mentioned, as business professionals focus their efforts on keeping up with technology, the little things I talk about have been increasingly falling off their radar screens and are in danger of falling off the face of the earth entirely.

How To Use This Book

First, please don't start out reading this book on a Sunday with the intention of blasting through it so that by Monday morning you will be the new super detail-oriented person who gets promoted next week. You may be able to read 601 little things that fast, but you can't possibly begin to work them all into your life overnight. You may discover that you have some bad habits to break and that may take time. Even if you don't have a habit to break, creating a good habit can take time, too.

So my advice is to read through this book section by section with an open mind. Focus first on the areas where you know you need help or aren't sure if you do. Each day, try to pay attention to a few of the essential things you've read. Try them out.

I do caution you not to dismiss anything until you've tried to incorporate it into your working day. Don't just say, "Well, I do that," or "I would never do that." I've coached and trained a really frightening number of people who routinely tell me, "I had no idea I did that!" A woman swore in my class that she did not stand passively—legs crossed and often resting on one ankle. "I never do that," she declared. Yet sure enough she was shocked during the break when I pointed to her feet and they were indeed crossed. She was speechless.

And that's because it's very easy not to know what you're doing when you've been doing it for a long time.

Some of the little things, as you will see, are pretty simple. For example: Say "Hello" and "Good morning," to your co-workers. But don't roll your eyes at the simplicity of this advice—at least until you try it. Don't just assume, "I'm sure I already do that." In fact, a startling number of people *don't* say hello and goodbye to their co-workers. This is exactly the kind of thing that *really* bugs people. People don't like to be ignored.

Still other little things will take some more time, like improving your writing skills or learning how to make small talk, if these aren't skills that come to you naturally. Just give it some time. Being mindful is your first big step to change.

Finally, at the end of this book, I've given you a top 20 list. These are the little things that, in my experience, are the most critical and can have the most immediate impact in changing your working life for the better. So if you want to jump in while you're reading through this whole book, this list is a good place to begin to take action.

Also at the end of this book you will find my e-mail and Web address. I love hearing your stories of how paying attention to the little things has changed or improved your working life.

I'm looking forward to hearing from you—and good luck!

❧ ONE ❧

BUILDING WORK RELATIONSHIPS
THAT WORK

*Graceful Greetings and Introductions * Shaking Hands Correctly * Learn
the Art of Making Small Talk * How to Listen to Others * Maintaining
Relationships with Your Co-workers * Office Romance Restrictions *
Networking Tips for Career Survival * Additional Guidelines for Business
Cards * Seven Networking Types You Don't Want to Become * Gift-Giving
Guidelines * Holiday Cards That Get You Noticed*

WELCOME TO A NEW business age. An age that is characterized
by dizzying change, the loss of job longevity and loyalty, and
lots of new technology.

Welcome to the uncertain business age.

But what hasn't changed, what has remained *exactly* the same
in today's business world, is the need to establish good and genuine relationships with others. The business relationships you
forge, with both those within your office and those outside of it,
are critically important to your on-going success, most especially
in this uncertain business age.

People do business with people. And most of us want to do
business with or work with others that they know, like and trust.
How you interact with others—and this includes little things like

greetings, making small talk, listening, and networking—will determine whether those beneficial relationships are formed or not.

Graceful Greetings and Introduction

"Claude was an engineer in our department who never acknowledged those of us on the administrative or support staff. He acted like we didn't exist. Sure enough, one day, Claude had an emergency. He needed a specific hard-to-get part and when he went to the support staff, guess what? When he needed our help, we acted like he didn't exist."

1. **When you arrive at work, greet others with "hello" or "good morning."** It's amazing that I have to give this simple guideline, but it's clear to me that I do. One of the complaints I hear the most often from employees about their managers and their co-workers is that many people don't bother to say "hello" or otherwise offer a simple greeting. I hear: "It's like I don't exist" or "she thinks she's so important..."

2. **Don't assume you are greeting people.** People think they do it, but they often don't! You need to pay attention to your own greeting behavior for a few days and *really* discover whether you're greeting people or not.

3. **Use the 10–5 rule.** One manager who worked at a resort in Phoenix was given the 10–5 rule during her training. If you see someone at 10 feet, you must acknowledge him or her. At 5 feet, you must say something: "hello," "good afternoon," etc. It's a good rule!

4. **Say goodbye.** Make sure you say "goodbye" or "have a good evening," to your co-workers before leaving for the day. Don't simply sneak out.

5. **Make introductions when appropriate.** If you are the host, it is your responsibility to introduce your guest to others. If you're joining a group, make sure that the person you are with knows the other people in the group. Mention the name of the person of highest rank first regardless of gender. (See numbers 138–149 for gender etiquette guidelines.)

6. **Add some information.** If appropriate, add a little information about the person after you say his or her name. For example, "Ms. Reilly is our new contact on Project S."

7. **Introduce yourself, if necessary.** If you're participating in a conversation and there's a person you don't know and no one offers to make an introduction, you should introduce yourself. Simply say, "I don't believe we've met. I'm John Jones."

8. **Don't panic if you forget a name.** When making an introduction if you forget someone's name, just be honest about it. It's better to admit it than to not make the introduction. You can say, "Excuse me, but your name has just escaped me…" or "I'm sorry, I've forgotten your name." It happens.

Shaking Hands Correctly

"My new client is a woman and she has the limpest handshake I have ever felt. Whenever we shake hands, I lose a little respect for her."

9. **Shake hands when meeting someone.** In the United States the handshake is the proper business greeting and if you want to be taken seriously you must shake hands. You should also shake hands when you see someone you haven't seen in a while and when you say goodbye. One woman was told by her boss that she got her job because she shook hands with him at the beginning of the job interview and at the end. He viewed it as an indication of her professionalism.

10. **Both men and women shake hands.**

11. **Shake hands correctly.** Extend your hand at a right angle with your thumb pointing up. Touch thumb joint to thumb joint. Once you make contact, put your thumb down gently. Wrap your fingers around the other person's palm. Two to three pumps is enough. Many people think they shake hands this way and are surprised to find out that it isn't when they test it.

12. **Apply firm pressure when you shake.** Your handshake should be firm but not be bone-breaking. Firm is important. How do you feel about someone if you shake his or her hand and it is limp or weak? Whether you like it or not, your handshake will convey your degree of professionalism to others. One man told me, "I don't want to do business with a particular vendor; he has a wimpy handshake."

13. **Say something when you shake hands.** You can acknowledge the person's name and say, "It's very nice to meet you, Mr. Jones" or simply "Hello Mary" or "Good to see you again."

Learn the Art of Small Talk

"One always speaks badly when one has nothing to say."
—Voltaire

14. **Think of small talk as a gateway to new relationships and maintaining the old ones.** Knowing how to start and keep a conversation going will allow you to meet others, get to know them, and build upon your network. "Small talk" does not mean "unimportant" or "silly."

15. **Be willing to make the first move.** For those of us not born with the "gift of the gab," making general conversation can be a conundrum—and a stressful one! Yet I have seen many business professionals overcome shyness and reticence simply by challenging themselves to move out of their comfort zone and talk to people. It will only get easier over time. Most people are friendly once you start talking with them.

16. **Have interesting topics to discuss.** Reading the daily newspaper, or news magazines, watching news shows on TV, reading your professional journals and even simply observing the world around you are all great sources for interesting topics you can discuss.

17. **Plan a "daily conversation starter."** For some people, the hardest part of making small talk can be starting the conversation. I suggest preparing a "daily conversation starter." This is an opening line that can be used to get a conversation going with just about anyone. The weather, if it is unusual, can be a good conversation starter: "Did the storm affect your commute?"

The environment you are in: "The speaker was excellent. Have you heard him before?" A self-revelation is another good way to start: "I saw the new movie last night. Have you had a chance to see it?" A sincere compliment can often break the ice: "The presentation by your group was excellent."

18. **Maintain the conversation.** Once you get started, keep the conversation going by referring to the last time the two of you were together, discussing items of interest to the other person or asking questions to draw the other person out.

19. **Don't go overboard.** You usually need to limit the amount of detail when describing something so you don't overwhelm the other person.

20. **Use humor wisely.** Humor can be a lifesaver in embarrassing or stressful situations. It can also enliven an otherwise dull conversation. But you can also bomb badly. You must use humor appropriately—especially in the workplace. You can accidentally offend someone and cause conflict if you're not careful. Never tell ethnic, sexist, religious, or racial jokes in order to break the ice.

21. **Take turns talking.** You don't want to monopolize the conversation. Remember that building a relationship often begins by expressing a genuine interest in others and you can often do this by letting the other person speak. A good conversation is one in which all parties can express themselves.

22. **Be willing to reveal yourself.** You do need to reveal yourself, at least a little bit. You can share personal information, such as you just started graduate school;

that is fine. But explaining that you were rejected at three schools and finally got the money together to attend is not necessary to share. Don't get too personal too quickly.

How to Listen to Others

"Whenever I had a conversation with my co-worker Jane, I could tell she wasn't listening. She would look over my shoulder, at papers in her hand....As soon as I would stop talking she would quickly change the subject. It was so annoying! I had to assemble a special team to work on a project and didn't choose her because of this. I heard through the grapevine that she was upset. I didn't want to upset her but I also didn't want someone on my team who didn't listen to me or others."

23. **Understand why you need to listen.** The old adage that you were given two ears and one mouth for a reason is absolutely true. You want to listen more than you speak. You cannot build and maintain genuine relationships unless you truly listen to others. This is another area where I hear a lot of complaints. People don't like it when others don't listen.

24. **Prepare yourself to listen.** You need a non-distracting environment. Close the door. Turn off any music. Pay attention to your internal distractions. If you're hungry it's hard to listen. If you have to go to the bathroom it is hard to listen.

25. **Pay attention to your body language.** Are you looking at the person? Do you have a pleasant expression on your

face? What are your arms saying? Are they crossed, indicating you are closed off, or relaxed at your side?

26. **Give the person your undivided attention.** Don't look at papers, open mail, or answer the telephone!

27. **Stop talking.** Let the other person talk! This is hard for many people. But trust me, you can't talk and listen at the same time.

28. **Don't interrupt.** People don't like to be interrupted. Not only is this rude, it shows you're not listening but planning what you're going to say next.

29. **Concentrate.** Try not to let your mind wander. Even if the person is boring. Pretend you have to report back on what you are hearing.

30. **Don't pre-judge someone.** Don't make assumptions about someone's ability to discuss a topic before you've had the discussion. If you are talking to an electrical engineer and he or she makes suggestions about the landscaping, you may be tempted to stop listening. But that person may know just what he or she is talking about when it comes to both subjects.

31. **Don't become "Technophobic" Tom or Tammy.** This is the person who stops listening or "shuts down" as a defense mechanism when things get too technological. Try to stay with the conversation; you just may learn something.

32. **Acknowledge that you are listening.** You can do this verbally by saying, "Oh," or "I see." Don't overuse them. You can offer a non-verbal acknowledgement too by occasionally nodding your head.

33. **Ask questions.** If you don't understand something or you want to get more information ask a question. It also lets the other person know you are listening and interested.

34. **Paraphrase what the other person is telling you.** Phrases such as "You're suggesting..." or "If I understand you correctly, you believe..." "What you're saying is...." Don't overdo this, but you do want the person to understand that you are listening and understanding what he or she is saying.

Maintaining Relationships with Your Co-Workers

"Jayne had left the department and didn't keep in touch with any-one—even though she was just in the next building. Then all of a sudden, she's looking for a job again and starts calling us. Where was she for the last two years?"

35. **Participate in company and department events.** Go to lunch with your group. Attend company parties. Contribute to group gifts. I know you are thinking you don't have time. You don't have to go to every party, but you do need to attend some of them. Even those little chats by the coffeepot or water cooler can help you maintain good office relationships and aren't just for gossip or goofing off. Those little impromptu gatherings are often important for creating that positive work/social environment that allows relationships to be maintained.

36. **Don't get too personal.** You want to know a little about your co-workers' lives, but you don't need to

know everything. You also need to talk about your life, but again, keep it simple. You want to maintain your relationships by showing consideration, interest and appreciation for others. These simple little things will go a long way toward making the workplace a more pleasant and productive place to be—for you and for everyone around you.

37. **Share.** Respect your co-workers' space and time. When using conference rooms or equipment, such as copiers, faxes and coffee machines, think of the others who will be using them after you. Clean up after yourself. Make sure supplies are in order.

38. **Help others.** If a co-worker needs some help and you can do it, why not offer your assistance?

39. **Use polite language.** I know you know you're supposed to do it, but we don't always take the time to say such simple words as "please" "thank you," or "I appreciate your effort."

40. **Offer sincere compliments.** If someone does an outstanding job, initiates an innovative idea, offers a unique suggestion, etc., tell the person what you think.

41. **Don't gossip.** You will get a reputation if you do. People may not trust you to keep confidences.

42. **Don't be a complainer.** If all you do is complain about work, other co-workers, etc., you will not be someone other people want to be around. Complainers are draining!

43. **Return phone calls and e-mails.** Don't just get back to your clients promptly, your co-workers count too. Again, no one likes to be ignored.

Office Romance Restrictions

"Everyone said, 'Don't date your boss,' and now I wish I had listened. I did date my boss, it didn't work out and now I can't work with him, much less for him. Even though I love my job I plan on leaving."

44. **Think carefully before you date someone at work.**
    Work is the place where more and more people meet their mates, because that's where we spend most of our time—but be careful. Office romances can have a big and—if not handled correctly—a negative impact not only on your professional relationship with the person you're dating but your performance and image as well.

45. **Don't date your boss.** Relationships are tricky enough without this kind of complication. You can't report to someone or effectively manage someone you're in love or sleeping with. But if this does occur you need to have your reporting relationship changed.

46. **Keep the relationship private.** Don't broadcast that you're dating someone. Even if your company takes a liberal view of office romance it just isn't professional to share details—good or bad—with others you work with. Send any cards, gifts, or flowers to the home, not the office.

47. **No physical contact in the office.** No secret kissing, caressing, hand holding or sex in the office. People get caught and careers can get ruined.

48. **Business rules apply in business-related social functions.** At the office party or any business social func-

tion do not drink too much, wear seductive clothing, do not dance too closely, and no seductive language.

49. **If the relationship fails—be professional and adult about it.** Even if you've been jilted and the relationship ends badly you cannot vent your negative feelings in the office. This is the risk of office relationships. They sometimes don't work out and then you have to see the person every day.

Networking Tips For Career Survival

"I am a naturally shy person but I forced myself to practice the tips from the networking class so I talked to the person next to me on the plane. Not only did we hit it off and have a great conversation but as it turns out her husband was leading the research project that I'm working on. I got invited to their house for a barbecue. It gave me the chance to talk with him and share my ideas, some of which he really liked. As a result of that one conversation, I got an incredibly more visible role in the project."

50. **Understand that because networking is about forming honest, sincere relationships, there's more involved than just "working a room" or "doing lunch."** Networking is about connecting with others in all areas of your life. It's about forming relationships that can benefit you, the other person, your careers and your lives. These relationships not only connect you with people, but with new ideas and information, strategic partnerships, better business practices, job opportunities, potential customers, clients and vendors.

51. **Form both an internal and external network.** You need both. Your network is internal (within your company) *and* external (other companies, same profession or other professions). Your network will be filled with people you know professionally *and* socially. And if you are successful in nurturing and maintaining your network, they will often merge. Ideally, your network can support you in business *and* support you in your personal life.

52. **Start with a positive attitude.** Consider your network as a part of your job and career, not an add-on if you have time. Think of it as a way to ensure some stability in your career in an uncertain business age.

53. **Be open.** Understand that in order to truly "connect" with others in a genuine way, you must be open, honest and interested in others. Seek help from others, but offer to help in return.

54. **Challenge yourself.** If you're shy, you may have to venture out of your comfort zone. I have coached many, many professionals and with time and practice I have witnessed shy people, even phobic people, network successfully, and even truly enjoy it! If they can do it, you can too.

55. **Make an effort to meet new people.** Get out of your office and off the telephone. Attend business and social functions. Volunteer at the office, especially for cross-departmental activities. Join company teams. You don't have to be a great softball player. Just get out there and have fun. Connecting over the telephone and via e-mail is effective, but you still need to get out and meet real live people.

56. **Specialize.** Become an expert on a particular topic so others will seek you out. Get published on your area of expertise. Submit articles to you local newspapers, magazines, and trade publications. Write an article for your company newsletter.

57. **Join professional, community and philanthropic organizations.** Volunteer for the committees. That's the way you get to know people and they get to know you.

58. **Diversify your network.** Look for places and events to meet people who are completely outside your immediate profession but are in an area that interests you or have skills that you don't have but would like to have or explore. Having more than one bankable skill set is critical today. I know a stockbroker who got laid off after on-line trading became popular. He always liked to write and was good at it. He was smart enough to have people in his network who could help him land a job writing about finance for a magazine. He doesn't make as much money but he's happier and doesn't worry about being outclassed by technology.

59. **Take advantage of every opportunity.** Consider every person you come in contact with as a potential member of your network.

60. **Nurture your network.** You need to stay in touch with people. Join colleagues for lunch. E-mail is a really convenient way to stay in touch, but don't abuse this by adding the person to your joke list. If you promised to send someone something, do it promptly. Send holiday cards. Clip articles and send them to people in your network. Be on the look-out for ways to solve problems for people.

61. **Socialize outside of the office.** Networking means you must actively socialize and interact with others outside of the office—at dinners, meetings, retreats, events or activities.

62. **Before any social engagement, prepare your self-introduction.** This is your ten-second commercial. It's your name and two to three sentences summarizing who you are and what you do. Tailor it to each event. Think about items that would be interesting to discuss also.

63. **Have an opening line you feel comfortable with, such as "This is a wonderful buffet. The food looks fantastic."** Or, ask an open-ended question to get a conversation started, such as, "How long have you been a member of the association?"

64. **Know how to enter a room.** You need to arrive on time. Walk into the room as if you belong there and know several people there, even if you don't. Get an overview of the room. Greet the hosts. Look for someone you know that you can easily approach. If you don't know anyone, look for someone standing alone and walk up and start a conversation. Generally, a person standing alone will be happy to be approached.

65. **Introduce yourself and shake hands.** Review the guidelines listed above. Hold your drink in your left hand so the right is always free and dry for shaking hands.

66. **Be genuinely interested in others.** Listen to what someone else is saying. Acknowledge that you are listening by maintaining eye contact and nodding. The point isn't to introduce yourself and make a hasty exit. The point is to make personal business connections with others.

67. **Mingle.** Challenge yourself to move out of your comfort zone. You are supposed to circulate and meet new people.

68. **Exchange business cards.** Make sure you attend any potential networking event well stocked with your business cards. The goal isn't to burn through a box of cards, but to give someone who you would like to be part of your network a tangible way to remember you.

69. **Ask for someone's business card.** Generally if you want to give someone your card and he or she hasn't asked for it, ask for his or hers. You will usually end up exchanging cards then. Shortly after parting, make a note on the person's card to remind yourself about who the person is and if and when you promised to contact him or her in the future.

70. **Have a system for business cards.** Put the cards you receive in one pocket and the ones you are giving out in another. That way you won't give out someone else's card.

ADDITIONAL GUIDELINES FOR BUSINESS CARDS:

71. **Stay current.** Have cards that are up to date. Do not cross out your address and hand write your new address.

72. **Use a card case.** A good quality card case looks professional and will help keep your business cards in good condition. You don't want to be digging cards out from the bottom of your purse or briefcase.

73. **Be prepared.** Carry cards with you all the time. You don't have to give them out everywhere you go, but you don't want to be without them if you need them.

74. Know when to give them out. Generally you exchange cards at the end of the conversation or the meeting. But people do also exchange cards at the beginning of a meeting. It's a great way to help you remember the person's name.

SEVEN NETWORKING TYPES YOU DON'T WANT TO BECOME

Attending a professional event or a business social gathering gives you the opportunity to build upon a valuable asset—your professional network. In order to be a successful networker, you need to be willing to "put yourself out there" and show a genuine interest in others. Below are seven types of networkers who make the worst impression. Some try too hard; others don't try hard enough.

#1. THE THERE'S-SOMEONE-ELSE-I'D-RATHER-BE-TALKING-TO is the one with a roving eye. He or she may be talking to you, but is obviously looking around the room or at someone else.

#2. Look out for the TERMINATOR. He doesn't shake hands, he crushes them. He invades other people's "space" too. This is a person you want to escape from. (Women are Terminators too!)

#3. NICE-MEETING-YOU-GOTTA-RUN is the fast-talker who doesn't just "work" the room, he or she burns holes in the carpet. He or she can burn through a box of business cards in a week, but makes no effort to establish meaningful business and personal relationships with others.

#4. MS. MELROSE PLACE dresses inappropriately in skin-tight or low-cut clothing. You see her flinging her long hair to and fro and wonder what she's really selling. MR. MELROSE PLACE undresses every woman with his eyes and loves stealing glances at this own reflection.

#5. You'll recognize the I-WISH-THIS-WALL-COULD-SWALLOW-ME-WHOLE networker not only by his or her tendency to hide in a corner against a wall, but by his or her bad body language: arms folded across the chest, shoulders hunched and/or her feet crossed at the ankles. This person won't talk much and seems uninterested when others do.

#6. THE I'M-THE-GREATEST-THING-SINCE-THE-INTERNET networkers love to hear themselves talk. They're distracted and bored when they're not the center of attention. They rarely show genuine interest in others.

#7. There's always at least one YOU-CAN-ONLY-CONNECT-WITH-ME-VIA-E-MAIL networker. This person doesn't understand that e-mail is not a replacement for human contact.

Gift-Giving Guidelines

"I was really pleased that the decorator for the office gave us a beautiful plant when she finished the job—until I found a note under one of the leaves that indicated the plant had originally been given to her!"

75. **Understand that gifts can have an impact on your work relationships.** A nighttime word processor for a law firm told me that she rarely sees or interacts with the attorneys she does work for because of her hours. But she takes especially good care of one of the firm's attorney's because he was the only one who left her a holiday gift and card on her chair. It wasn't a huge or expensive gift; it really was the thought that counted.

76. **Know the different types of gifts and when it's appropriate to give them.** Business gifts are generally exchanged among company employees, clients, cus-

tomers or vendors to celebrate birthdays, holidays, retirements, births, or to thank someone. Hostess gifts are given when you go to someone's home for a meal or party. Hostess gifts are required. Business gifts depend upon the relationship between the giver and receiver and company policy.

77. **Employee gifts.** An employee is not required to give a boss a gift. A boss can give an employee a gift. In some companies a department will "chip in" and buy a group gift for a boss.

78. **Don't send the wrong message.** Be careful about giving gag gifts or gifts that aren't appropriate for any type of business gift giving, like nightgowns, which have a romantic connotation.

79. **Simple often works best.** You want to choose a quality item, but it doesn't mean you have to spend a fortune or buy something complicated. Choose a gift with the particular person in mind. If you're uncertain about what to buy someone, here are some business gift ideas: Food—homemade cookies are generally an appreciated gift—business books, pocket calendar, holiday plants, pen and pencil sets, stationery or calculators. Taking the person to lunch can also be a nice and appropriate gift.

80. **Participate in company gift-giving traditions.** Some holiday gift giving is determined by company tradition, like "grab bags" with dollar limits. It's usually best to be part of the group and participate. It's important for you to know what kinds of gifts people give one another and to adhere to dollar limits.

81. **Know your company's guidelines for client/customer gift giving.** Many companies establish guidelines on

what is acceptable for employees to give their clients or customers and how much money can be spent on the gift. Depending upon your situation and relationship, it can be appropriate to give a client theater tickets, tickets to sporting events, or to treat them to a nice dinner. If your company has no such guidelines, check with your boss.

82. **Know your company's policy for gift receiving.** Some companies might not allow you to receive gifts from vendors or set dollar limits on the value of gifts that employees may receive. Some companies have a policy that all gifts must be shared or given to the company gift bank. A traffic manager once took home a whole tray of holiday cookies sent to him by a vendor. The vendor happened to meet the man's boss and asked him if he and the department enjoyed his gift.

83. **Hostess gifts.** A hostess gift, such as flowers, a gift set of assorted coffees, or a box of chocolates is required if you're attending a meal or party at a co-worker's or manager's home. If you give flowers, send them ahead of time so the hostess doesn't have to handle them when you arrive.

84. **Don't exaggerate.** Don't put a gift in a box from a fancy store if it doesn't come from that store. If the person goes to return the item, he or she could be embarrassed. Don't pass off a gift that you don't want to someone else.

85. **Refuse graciously if you must.** If you must refuse a gift because accepting it would violate your company's policy, you don't ever want to embarrass the sender. Be gracious but explain why you cannot accept the gift. You can say, "How nice of you! Unfortunately, our

company policy prohibits me from accepting your thoughtful gift."

86. **Always send a thank-you note.** Even if you thank the giver in person, proper business etiquette calls for sending a thank-you note.

Holiday Cards That Get You Noticed

"A vendor sent a holiday card. It was a nice gesture, but he blew it when he used a pre-printed card and forgot to sign it. His competition wrote a very nice note on their card."

87. **Take the time to send holiday cards.** Sending holiday cards is an easy but very effective way to maintain relationships, get your name and your company name in front of potential clients, to remind existing clients that you appreciate their business, and to thank vendors for a job well done.

88. **Don't choose a religious theme.** Choose a card that expresses best wishes for a general holiday season rather than Christmas or Hanukkah specifically.

89. **Personalize your greeting.** If your name is printed on the card, be sure to write a quick note by hand, to personalize your greeting, and sign it.

90. **Personalize the envelope.** Don't use computer-generated labels to address your cards, it's too impersonal. Handwrite them—or have someone do it for you.

91. **Use stamps.** Holiday stamps rather than the company postal meter add a nice personal touch.

92. **Sympathy cards can also be important to send.** Make sure you include a personal note and a signature.

❧ TWO ❧

OFFICE SKILLS FOR THE NEW MILLENNIUM

*Meeting Manners that Matter * Home Office/Telecommuting Success **
*Polished Presentation Skills * Gender Etiquette Essentials*

TODAY, WITH TECHNOLOGY connecting us, it really doesn't matter where you're doing your business. Your office might be in a skyscraper or it could be in your extra bedroom. These days, people make million-dollar deals from home while still in their pajamas. But make no mistake, how you do your business matters more than ever. In order to be successful in this new business world, you still need to have great office skills.

In this section, I highlight the essential things of four key skill areas that today's professionals need to pay attention to—meetings, home office skills, presentation skills and gender etiquette issues. Some of the little things I highlight are fairly basic and haven't changed much year after year, like your meeting manners or your ability to make a good presentation. Other issues are still evolving, like gender etiquette, especially as more women than ever are moving into upper management levels. And still others, like home office success, didn't even seem to exist until a few years ago. Remember when working out of your house had a stigma attached to it? Now it's a status symbol!

The one important thing these four skill areas have in common— whether business as usual or new to the business world—they all frequently invite mistakes. You might, for example, think that simply showing your face at the weekly marketing meeting is enough to make you look good or that a woman not standing when greeting others isn't really that big of a deal. Well, think again! You not only need to show up at the weekly meeting, you need to participate effectively. Women not only need to stand upon greeting colleagues, but both men and women need to shake hands correctly.

Paying attention to the following items will help you improve your office skills in this ever-changing business world. Welcome to the new millennium!

Meeting Manners That Really Matter

"I arrived with my co-worker before the meeting began and was surprised to see the president of our company was attending. My co-worker immediately went up to the president, introduced himself and shook his hand. They had a brief conversation. Frankly, I thought my co-worker was being pushy. Then, twice during the meeting, the president asked him two questions directly—both on areas I could have contributed to in the conversation as well. About a month later, the president called him and asked him to take on a special project. Now I realize that I should have introduced myself too. I will the next time!"

93. Greet office staff upon your arrival. If you're attending a meeting in your organization's home or regional office and you don't know the secretaries and other administrative staff, always, always introduce yourself. Be friendly. People don't like to be ignored—they become angry, hurt or upset. Failing to show this simple interest in others can make your job harder down the road when you're calling for help or information. Always make a point to offer a greeting at subsequent office visits.

94. **Greet the other participants.** As the participants arrive, you should greet each person, even if you see them on a regular basis. Make a point to introduce yourself to any person you're not acquainted with. Remember, this could be your opportunity to meet that elusive vice president or to chat with the director of your region.

95. **Arrive on time.** It's rude and disrespectful to the other participants to arrive late and disrupt the proceedings.

96. **Don't groom yourself.** This is like taking a gun to your professional image and pulling the trigger. Why do people believe it's acceptable to put on lipstick, comb hair, clip fingernails, manicure or bite fingernails while at a meeting table? It's completely unacceptable and, unfortunately, it happens all the time. Grooming during a meeting is considered gross behavior by many others. You will be remembered for it.

97. **Maintain proper posture.** Don't put your feet up, lean on the table, or slouch over. You may seem disrespectful, as though you don't care about what's being said or you're not paying attention.

98. **Pay attention.** I know a very smart computer consultant who was reprimanded after a meeting by a partner in

his organization—who wasn't even his boss—for reading his e-mails on his laptop. Don't read e-mail and memos—unless they pertain to the matter being discussed. Don't work on your laptop or your electronic organizer. Twisting paperclips, doodling and biting pencils—all bad habits—will give others the impression that you aren't paying attention. Keep side conversations to a minimum.

99. **Prepare for your part of the meeting.** If you don't, you will look like the kid who gets caught not doing his or her homework. "Kids" usually don't get the next high profile project or the big year-end bonus.

100. **Be an enthusiastic participant.** You don't have to solve every problem or make a breakthrough suggestion at every meeting. But you do have to participate in order to make a good impression, share information, learn and be a team player.

101. **Turn off cell phones and beepers.** Unless you're expecting an emergency call, such as your wife is expecting a baby at any minute, turn them off or put them on vibrate. If you do take a call, excuse yourself from the room. A woman when introducing a speaker answered her cell phone and proceeded to talk. She finished the conversation and went back to her introduction. That is not okay!

102. **Let others have their say.** Don't dominate the conversation. Interrupting others is probably one of the fastest ways to get labeled as an annoying person. People don't like it when others don't listen. If you are running the meeting, try to bring everyone into the conversation.

103. **Stay for the entire meeting.** Only leave a meeting early if it simply can't be avoided. Tell the other participants

in the beginning that you will be leaving at a specific time and apologize in advance for any inconvenience this may cause.

104. **Clean up after yourself.** Throw away your discarded papers and any soda cans and trash you may have generated. It's rude and thoughtless to assume that someone else will clean up your mess.

Home Office / Telecommuting Success

"I was about to give a big project to a woman who was running a PR business out of her office. During our conversation, her eight-year-old son started screaming to her in the background. She started screaming back at him. I didn't give her the job because I was worried she would get on the phone with media people and do the same thing while pitching our product."

105. **Have a separate space for your office.** You need an area or room that is private and with a door that closes. You need to be assured that you won't hear dogs barking, your neighbor's lawn mower or your children playing. And if you have children, establish a closed-door policy. Your children need to know that you are working and unless it's an emergency or really important, they are not to disturb you. My son Jacob, when he was a toddler, once screamed out while I was on the phone, "Mommy, I fell in the potty!" Try to explain that to a potential client at a Fortune 100 company!

106. **Use a dedicated phone line for business.** You don't want to be sharing the phone with others at home and

have to wait to get on the line or have other people pick up the phone by mistake while you're talking.

107. **Answer your phone professionally.** Give a greeting, your name and company. For example: "Good morning, Pachter & Associates, this is Barbara Pachter."

108. **Invest in a good answering system.** I suggest a voice mail system so you can access your messages away from home. Also have your callers hear a good quality professional message—no little kids talking or music blasting. Tell them who they have reached and when you will return the call.

109. **Don't use call waiting in business.** It's incredibly rude and disruptive to the caller and you.

110. **Use a dedicated fax line.** It's more convenient for people to send you faxes this way. It creates a more professional impression. Make sure you're using a fax cover sheet with your company information as well.

111. **Dress up if you need to.** When I first started working at home, I would dress as if I was going to an office. I felt more professional. Many people with home offices tell me the same thing. However, if you can work well in your PJs, as long as you don't videoconference, go for it!

112. **Have the appropriate space if you meet with people at your home office.** This also applies if you have a meal during the meeting. If you don't have the space, arrange the use of a meeting room or meet at a restaurant or cafe.

113. **Establish rapport with workers at your company's office.** You don't want to be forgotten. You still need to go see them. Send birthday cards, make an effort to

appear at the office parties, and make lunch dates with your colleagues.

114. **Keep your car in good shape.** Your car is an extension of your office. And you may still be driving with clients, vendors, co-workers or bosses. The car needs to be clean with no trash or toys. A woman I know was very embarrassed when she picked up her mentor for lunch and he found dog bones on his seat!

115. **Get good quality business cards and stationery, if you're in business for yourself.** Use a post office box. Get a website. These are all indications that you're a serious professional.

Polished Presentation Skills

"I thought I gave great speeches and presentations—until my boss told me he thought I needed to brush up on my public speaking skills, especially if I wanted to be considered to give the big presentation at the next trade show. I was really mad at him until I had myself videotaped. Every other word out of my mouth was 'Um.' I had no idea I did this."

116. **View stage fright as positive energy.** When you make presentations, you would probably flop without at least one or two butterflies fluttering around in your stomach. You need adrenaline and energy to perform well. This is true because stage fright is really just a form of energy (a by-product of your adrenaline) and if you didn't have this energy flowing through your body your presentation would be flat and lifeless. So the first trick

in overcoming stage fright is to stop thinking of it as a negative thing. Understand that without it, athletes wouldn't win, campers wouldn't outrun bears and your presentation wouldn't be terrific.

117. **Prepare.** Preparation is the key to feeling confident. If you know your subject and know what you are going to be talking about, you will be less fearful. Make sure you organize your speech and prepare your notes ahead of time.

118. **Practice. Practice. Practice.** You need to practice your presentation several times. You will be giving your presentation by speaking it so you need to practice by speaking it too. And practice it out loud. The more you hear yourself saying the words the more confident you will become in your delivery.

119. **Have a dress rehearsal.** Do a complete run through of your whole presentation, preferably in the actual place you will be giving it. Ask a few friends or co-workers to attend. For many, the first time is the worst time so get it over with. This will also help you discover if you have any glitches or problems that need to be corrected. Ask your audience members for feedback and be open to their comments.

120. **Dress appropriately.** You want to be viewed as a credible source and your clothing can help. Generally, the business suit for both men and women is the most appropriate outfit for a professional office presentation. Darker colors convey more authority. Both men and women need to keep double-breasted jackets buttoned. Men: Keep your single-breasted jackets buttoned. Women: Don't wear hanging earrings that sway and bracelets that jangle when you move.

121. Arrive early. Give yourself plenty of time to set up equipment, arrange visual aids, correct problems and greet participants. You won't just look "in control," you will be "in control."

THE FIVE WORST THINGS I'VE SEEN DURING A PRESENTATION

I've been asked to critique or have been an audience member for quite a few presentations. I've witnessed a wide range of mistakes, flops and blunders—and dozens of flies that were unfortunately down—it really does happen all the time. Besides the CEO's fly being down, here are the five worst things I've seen during a presentation:

#1. The woman who presented with a giant—I mean giant—run in her stockings. (She should have checked and had an extra pair on hand.)

#2. A manager who told a joke with a nun in it. (And it wasn't funny.)

#3. The very successful venture capitalist who licked his lips repeatedly. (I wanted to toss lip balm onto the stage.)

#4. A lecturer who stopped every two minutes and drank from a bottle of water. (This was a forty-minute presentation.)

#5. The VP who beat herself on the leg with a pointer during a presentation. (I wondered if she bruised herself!)

All of these things above, though all accidents or habits, distracted or otherwise turned off the audience—that's why even innocent mistakes can work against you. The kiss of death to any presentation is when your audience's attention is led elsewhere or if you lose your credibility the moment you appear before your audience. If you are a person who must give frequent presentations, I encourage you to take the self-assessment I've included and to study and practice the 22 essential details you need to pay attention to for making polished presentations.

122. Fake it until you feel it. If you know your material and understand how to use your verbal and non-verbal skills effectively, you won't look nervous even if there's an earthquake going on inside you. You will seem poised and confident to your audience. Most people find that sooner or later the feeling will catch up to the appearance.

123. Organize your presentation correctly. Every presentation should have three separate and distinguishable parts: the introduction, the main body and the conclusion.

124. Use an attention-getting introduction. Make an unexpected statement, quote a prominent figure, cite a relevant statistic, tell an interesting story, ask questions, etc. For example, "Five people in this room will be diagnosed with a serious medical condition by the time they retire" or "If they say you can't get rich quick then how did Joe Smith do it in less than one year?"

125. Have a definite purpose. In your introduction let the audience know what you will be talking about.

126. If no one introduces you, introduce yourself. Briefly explain to your audience why you are qualified to speak on the topic.

127. Be cautious with humor. Humor can make you a hero with your audience or it can make them wish they had some tomatoes on hand. If you're going to use humor, it should never be at anyone's expense. Never tell a joke that has to do with sex, religion or politics.

PRESENTATION SKILLS SELF-ASSESSMENT

#1. I look at people in the audience when speaking.

#2. My facial expression is consistent with what I am saying.

#3. I do not point my finger or pound on a table.

#4. I speak loudly enough for others to hear.

#5. When speaking, I do not play with my hair, tie or jewelry or crack my knuckles or play with change in my pockets.

#6. I avoid overusing filler words such as "OK," "All right," "You know," "Uh huh."

#7. I think about my audience when preparing the presentation.

#8. I prepare an introduction and a conclusion.

#9. My visual aids are simple and easy to read.

#10. I avoid reading from a manuscript.

Even if you only answered "No" to one of the ten questions above—you need to work on your presentation skills. Even just making one of these mistakes can cause you to lose credibility. Your presentation will suffer.

128. Make sure the body of the presentation has from three to five main points. Any more than that may be too much for your audience to absorb. Each point should be accompanied by supporting materials such as stories, illustrations, facts, statistics, or details.

129. Use an open posture. Stand with your legs approximately 4–6 inches apart. Your weight should be distributed evenly on both legs. Keep your shoulders back but remember, you're not in a military inspection. Your chin should be up but not dramatically so. And unless you're gesturing, your hands should remain at your sides. Do not sway.

130. Use gestures. Gestures bring your words to life so use them—but don't overuse them. Be aware not to use nervous gestures, like playing with a paperclip or twisting your hair.

131. **Be aware of your voice.** If-you-talk-in-one-tone-of-voice-your-audience-will-fall-asleep. Vary your pitch, volume and rate. Speak loudly enough to be heard in the back of the room.

132. **Make eye contact.** If you want to establish rapport with your audience, you need to look at them. Don't stare anyone down.

133. **Use assertive wording.** As I mention in detail number 203, self-discounting, non-authoritative language undermines your professional image. It also affects formal presentations. Don't use phases such as "I kinda, sorta maybe think that perhaps what I'm telling you will be helpful." "I think another thing I probably want to say is...." Use assertive language that conveys your authority: "This information will save you money."

134. **If you use visual aids, keep them simple.** They need to be visually appealing but not overdone. Use a title and bullet key items. And make sure you speak to the audience and not the visual aid. Know how to use the equipment. Practice giving the presentation using the equipment. And be prepared if the equipment doesn't work!

135. **Have an effective conclusion.** Remind your audience of what you have just told them. And you need to end with a provocative or memorable remark. Again, be cautious with your use of humor.

136. **Take questions.** Let the audience know when you will be taking questions. Repeat the question before you answer it. Anticipate the tough questions and know how you will answer them.

137. **Have yourself videotaped.** If you give frequent presentations or speeches, have yourself videotaped. I tell the

people I coach, "Don't tell me you don't have any distracting behaviors until you get feedback that you don't." People are often shocked and embarrassed when they see themselves in action. I hear, "I had no idea I did that" or "Why didn't anyone tell me I did that?"

Gender Etiquette Essentials

"I held the door for one of my female co-workers and boy did she get upset with me! She said she wasn't helpless and to not treat her that way. I thought I was just being nice."

THE RULES OF GREETINGS/INTRODUCTIONS:

138. **Realize the working world has changed.** Should a male co-worker hold the door for his female co-worker? Is it still appropriate to introduce women first? Does the man pay the bill? Whew...it has gotten confusing. The confusion largely stems from the practice of applying the social rules of etiquette to the workplace *and* ignorance of the new etiquette. The social rules—where men take care of women and pay deference to them simply because they are women—do not belong in the workplace. Some of these rules are disappearing from the social scene as well, but what people do in their private lives is up to them.

139. **Extending the hand.** In handshaking, it used to be that a man waited for a woman to extend her hand, but not anymore. The person who has the higher rank, regardless of gender, should extend his or her hand first. But

if he or she doesn't—often because of the gender confusion—you extend yours. You are establishing yourself as a professional when you do. (If you would like more information on how to shake hands, see numbers 9–13.)

140. **Standing when greeting others.** It used to be that a woman did not stand up when being introduced or when greeting others, but again, not anymore. Like their male counterparts, women should stand. In fact, women who don't stand upon greeting set themselves up to be at a disadvantage. If there are five men and one woman in a room and the CEO walks in and all the men stand and the woman doesn't, how is the CEO going to perceive her? She is going to seem unimportant and not a member of the group.

141. **Making an introduction.** When making an introduction it used to be that a woman's name was said first. Now, the name of the person of highest rank is said first. For example, "Mr. Greater Importance, I'd like you to meet Ms. Lesser Importance."

142. **Writing the salutation.** "Dear Sir" is now defunct as a generic salutation. "Dear Sir/Ms." is technically correct, but it is impersonal, and it is therefore less effective than a gender-neutral salutation such as "Dear Customer."

143. **Using Ms. as a general guideline.** "Ms." is the preferred term in business, but etiquette dictates that people should be addressed as they are comfortable. If someone tells you she prefers to be addressed as Miss, Ms. or Mrs. you should respect her request.

THE NEW RULES OF HELPING ETIQUETTE:

144. **Opening the door.** Whoever gets to the door first, regardless of gender, should open it. It's always good manners to hold the door for the person behind you.

145. **Ordering the food.** Men should no longer order for women. Each person should give his or her order to the waiter. If you are host, you should invite your guest of honor to order first. As a woman if the waiter comes up to you, you can say, "Oh, please take my guest's order first."

146. **Paying the bill.** The host should do the inviting and bill paying regardless of gender. If a man wants to pay the bill a woman does have some choices. She can excuse herself and pay the bill, she can say, "Oh, it's not me whose paying, it's ABC company." If a man really wants to pay, let him! You don't want to fight over a bill.

147. **Carrying packages.** It used to be that a man helped a woman carry packages, whether she needed assistance or not. Today, you should carry packages for anyone who needs or asks for your assistance.

148. **Putting on coats.** It used to be that men helped women on with their coats, but today, the rule is the same as the one above: help anyone who needs it, regardless of gender.

149. **Pulling out chairs.** Women can pull out their own chairs.

~ THREE ~

YOUR PROFESSIONAL PRESENCE

*Secrets of Professional Dress and Grooming * Dress and Grooming
Guidelines Just for Men * Dress and Grooming Guidelines Just for Women
* Business Casual Concerns * Body Language Basics * The Top Ten Most
Distracting Behaviors Every Professional Should Avoid * Sounding As
Good As You Look * Diction Dilemmas*

THANKFULLY, IT'S NOT a beauty contest out there in the world of work, but let's be realistic: How others "see" you matters. I don't mean whether they "see" you as a tall or short person or someone with straight or curly hair. I mean whether or not they "see" you as someone who has a polished professional appearance. Do others "see" you as someone who shows up for the important client meeting appropriately dressed or the person with a stain on his tie or a run in her stockings? Do others "see" you as the person who slinks down the hallway with your shoulders hunched as if you want the carpet to swallow you whole or the person who walks tall and commands respect?

Do others "see" you as someone with a terrific professional presence?

You might be tempted to think that how you wear your hair, how you stand, how you speak or how you dress on casual day are superficial details. You might think that it's your work, and only your work, that matters, but this simply isn't a realistic or smart attitude. Fair or not, we are all judged, to some degree, by how we put ourselves together, or fail to, each morning.

Jason, a chemist for a growing pharmaceutical company, was a very bright scientist who was doing innovative work. But frankly, he looked like a slob. His hair was uncombed. His clothes were usually wrinkled and sometimes stained. He didn't even wear socks all time!

Jason was asked to make himself look more presentable for meetings with investors and potential buyers. The president was worried that Jason's sloppy appearance was costing the entire company credibility. Jason arrogantly thought he was above minding these kinds of details and continued to disregard his professional appearance. When his company was purchased by a larger company, another chemist was made head of research. Jason was furious about being passed over. He quit about six months later.

Jason might be an extreme example, but I hear all kinds of stories every day about people who blow their credibility because they don't pay attention to the many essential things that make up their professional presence—the manager who speaks so softly no one can hear her or the sales director who wears shirts that are so tight, he popped a button during a client meeting!

You put these essential things together and they can work for your professional presence or against it. You want them to work for you!

Secrets of Professional Dress and Grooming

"Sally, one of our field representatives, showed up at the regional office on a hot summer day wearing a low-cut sleeveless blouse and very short skirt. We were shocked. We are a conservative organization and we thought Sally understood this. I lost all respect for her that day."

150. **Understand the importance of professional dress.** Managers and human resource personnel frequently tell me that their employees know the job and/or technical information, but they just don't look as credible or powerful as they need to in the clothing they choose to wear. Many, they say, are not promoted because of it.

151. **Ask yourself, "Is what I'm wearing appropriate?"** Is your clothing suitable for your job, profession, company, the event or activity that you're attending, the region of the country or the world that you're working in? Look around you and see how respected people in higher positions dress. You can usually take your cue from them. In many organizations, especially dotcoms and high-tech ventures, the dress code can be very casual. If you work for a casual company then you would probably feel out of place wearing a suit to the office. Just make sure that your causal wear is still appropriate. (See guidelines for business casual below.)

152. **Choose clothing that fits properly.** Your clothing needs to fit without over-emphasizing your body. Nothing should fit too tightly, and there shouldn't be any buttons pulling or bulging of fabric. Men need to be able to button their jackets and make sure their pants are long enough. Women need to be able to move their arms and must not expose things like cleavage.

153. **Buy the most expensive clothing you can afford.** You spend most of your time at work, so spend most of your clothing budget on work clothes. You don't need to buy a lot; you want to buy good-quality, classic clothing—nothing too trendy. It usually is made better, lasts longer, wears better and doesn't go out of style as quickly. Less really is more when it comes to professional clothing.

154. Know what message you're sending. What is your clothing saying about you? Does it project the image of a serious professional? If a man shows up at a meeting in business casual clothing, but every other man in the room is wearing a professional suit—what message is he sending? If a woman wears a sexy, tight, seductive dress to a company party, what message is she sending? You want to be viewed as someone who pays attention to the details and is ready for work.

155. When in doubt, choose a business suit. The business suit is still the most powerful look for both men and women. Darker colors convey more authority than lighter colors, but big men need to be cautious with black. It can be intimidating. If a woman wears very bright colors, she may draw too much attention to herself for the wrong reason.

156. Shoes matter. I've had numerous recruiters tell me that one of the first things they notice about a candidate is his or her shoes. One sales representative told me that as he was leaving the interview with his future boss, the boss said, "You didn't hear it from me, but I would lose those shoes!" Shoes should be polished and in good condition. Thinner-soled shoes are more elegant for men and a shoe with a lace is more appropriate when wearing a business suit. Women need to avoid very high heels—a 2" to 2 1/2" heel is appropriate.

157. Don't skimp on accessories. A good-quality leather briefcase, umbrella, and leather gloves are all a must. Buy the best watch you can afford. Handbags also should also be good quality.

158. Be prepared. In case of emergency keep mouthwash and dental floss in your office or desk drawer. Men should keep an electric razor for five o'clock shadow. Women should keep an extra pair of stockings and a nail file.

159. **Consider a personal shopper.** If you are uncomfortable choosing your own clothes, get help! Pick a good store and develop a relationship with their personal shopper. He or she will help you find clothes that are suited for you.

160. **Have a hairstyle.** Wear a style that is current and flatters your face. I had to tell one man I coached that his new spiked hairstyle was not appropriate for his Fortune 100 job!

161. **Don't break the rules out of ignorance.** You can break all these guidelines, but you can't break them out of ignorance. You must know that you can pull it off. And don't you just tell me you can pull it off, you must get feedback from others that you can. The founder of Ikea Ingvar Kamprad's standard business attire is open-necked denim shirts. That is very different from most heads of companies. He has a personal fortune of about three billion dollars. He is obviously pulling it off!

DRESS AND GROOMING GUIDELINES JUST FOR MEN:

162. **Professional dress for men includes the two-piece suit and the sport coat with trousers.**

163. **Shirt sleeve should extend 1/8" to 1/4" below the jacket.** Make sure your collars are pressed.

164. **The tip of the tie should end at the middle of the belt.**

165. **Trouser legs should break at the front and taper down in the back.** And your pockets shouldn't bulge.

166. Socks need to cover calves.

167. Use braces, not clip-on suspenders. Do not wear braces with a belt. Belt color should match your shoe color.

168. No five o'clock shadow.

169. Limit the amount of aftershave you use. You don't want to be remembered for it long after you leave the room.

DRESS AND GROOMING GUIDELINES JUST FOR WOMEN:

170. Don't dress to be sexy! Showing too much leg (even really good ones) and revealing cleavage (no matter the size of your breasts) is never an appropriate way to dress for the office. This is the kind of mistake that can severely damage a woman's credibility in the workplace. Skirts should be worn no higher than the top of your knee and no cleavage should be showing.

171. Professional dress for women includes the skirt suit, the pantsuit, the unmatched suit and the one- or two-piece dress.

172. Belts should be leather and should coordinate with shoes.

173. Long hair on women in the workplace is too girlish, sexy, or distracting. If you choose to wear long hair, pull it back or put it up.

174. Very long nails, or nails with designs on them, are not appropriate for work.

175. Do not wear dark stockings with light shoes.

176. Wear a slip when appropriate. Make sure it doesn't show, especially when wearing a skirt with a slit.

177. **Wear a sleeveless blouse** *only under a jacket.*

178. **Jewelry should be of good quality.** Avoid long, hanging earrings and noisy jewelry. One ring per hand.

179. **Limit the amount of perfume you use.** You don't want to be remembered for it long after you leave the room.

Business Casual Concerns

"We had to revoke our casual business dress policy because employees were showing up in jeans with holes in them, stretch pants, and cartoon t-shirts despite numerous memos on the subject. It's like every one lost their common sense."

180. **Understand that casual does not mean sloppy!** Casual or not, clothing still needs to be clean and pressed and should fit properly. I hear numerous complaints about employees who abuse the business casual dress code by showing up in inappropriate attire.

181. **Know your company's policy.** If you're not clearly told what you're allowed to wear then ask your boss or someone in human resources. If your company policy allows jeans, they should be in good condition. Don't wear a worn-out, tattered pair with holes at the knee. Wear a belt.

182. **Think about your schedule when choosing your clothes.** If you are meeting with clients in their professionally dressed office, wear a professional suit. If your client company's wears business casual, decide whether it is appropriate for you to wear business casual or if

you should maintain the more professional look. Many professionals keep professional business clothes in their offices for emergencies so they are never caught unprepared.

183. **Avoid unprofessional attire.** Sweatpants, sweatshirts, shorts, tank or tube tops, halter tops and spandex or stirrup pants, spaghetti straps or strapless dresses are never appropriate for the office. Also, no holes, worn fabric or frayed collars. If your favorite sweater that your aunt gave you has holes where the elbows once were and is missing buttons, this article of clothing does not send the right message! Save it for weekends.

184. **Make sure your shoes are professional.** Sneakers, athletic shoes, flip-flops and slippers are not okay for the office.

185. **Good business casual for men includes: trousers and sport jacket or sweater, khakis or Dockers and a polo shirt.**

186. **Good business casual for women includes: dress; dress with jacket; pants, skirt or long skirt with blouse, sweater set or jacket.** (The jacket makes the woman look professional even though she is casually dressed.)

187. **Do participate on casual dress days.** Unless you're meeting a client, don't wear professional dress if the rest of your company is dressing casually. You will stand out for the wrong reason.

188. **When in doubt, leave it out.** If you are unsure whether it is appropriate, don't wear it.

189. **Dress appropriately for recreational activities at work.** Even at the company picnic or softball game, your clothing still matters. The key thing to remember is that it is still a business situation. No skimpy shorts, bathing suits, halter tops, muscle t-shirts, or ripped or

torn t-shirts. A woman manager lost her credibility when she showed up at the company pool party in a thong bathing suit!

Body Language Basics

"I had this habit of pounding my fist on the table when I was making a point. I thought it was a 'power' gesture and that it would make me seem confident. At my yearly review my boss told me that I was doing a great job but that I was too aggressive in meetings. She said I often seemed angry when making a point!"

190. **Tune into your body language.** Your non-verbal communication has a huge impact on your professional presence. Be careful! Many aspects of body language, such as gestures and posture, can become deeply ingrained habits—bad ones. Do you know when you're slouching or twisting your hair? Most people don't. So if you want to send a positive message about yourself, pay attention to your body language, get feedback from others and follow these guidelines.

191. **Watch out for negative gestures.** Don't wring your hands, cross your arms or point your finger or pound your fist to reinforce points.

192. **Stand tall.** No slouching, swaying or shifting feet.

193. **Sit tall.** Sit up straight. Don't shift or slouch in your seat, this makes it seem like you're not paying attention or that you feel uncomfortable. Don't tap your feet, this can imply impatience. Crossing your legs is bad for your circulation. You can cross your legs at the ankles.

194. **Maintain proper eye contact.** You need to look people in the eye, but don't stare them down. You do occasionally look away. But if you mostly look away, it will be perceived that you are not listening or are nervous. If you are talking to a group of people, make sure you make eye contact with everyone.

195. **Move with confidence.** When you walk, do so purposefully, as if you belong. Keep your chin up and your shoulders back. Try to maintain an even, deliberate stride. Don't drag or shuffle your feet. Make sure you don't point your feet outward when you walk. It's hard to be confident when you look like a duck. People will often tell me, "I knew you were the instructor by the confident way you walked into the room. You acted like you were in charge."

196. **Know your distance.** In the U.S., average distance between two people in business is approximately three feet or arms length. When speaking with others, don't stand too close. It can be intimidating to them.

197. **Be cautious with touch.** In today's world of sexual harassment we simply say, "Don't touch others." I know it is not always a harassment issue. There are touchy people, touchy professions and touchy cultures. But you still need to be cautious.

198. **Be aware of your facial expressions.** An engineer I met said that he was constantly being asked, "What's wrong?" when nothing was wrong. After just speaking with him for a couple of minutes, I knew why. He appeared to have a permanent frown on his face. Try to keep a pleasant expression on your face. Don't frown, stare or shift your eyes. Be animated. Wear a smile if and when appropriate.

THE TOP TEN MOST DISTRACTING BEHAVIORS
EVERY PROFESSIONAL SHOULD AVOID

I once coached an executive who scratched his face when he spoke. He saw himself on videotape and said, "I had no idea I did that when I was giving speeches." He was even more surprised when I told him that he did it all the time. It's so easy to adopt a distracting behavior and not even know it. So don't tell me you don't do these things until you get feedback that you don't!

#1. Pulling or playing with your hair.
#2. Playing with rubber bands or paper clips.
#3. Twirling your mustache.
#4. Drumming your fingers.
#5. Clicking pens.
#6. Licking or biting your lips.
#7. Picking or biting your fingernails.
#8. Tapping your feet.
#9. Picking your teeth.
#10. Adjusting your glasses.

Sounding As Good As You Look

"When I met customers, I felt like they weren't taking me seriously. I went to Barbara Pachter for help. She made me realize that I was too soft-spoken and that I had a habit of giggling at the end of my sentences. Now, I speak up and I don't giggle. I'm aware of how I sound and I am treated as a professional."

How You Say It:

199. Speak loudly enough to be heard. Many people speak too softly. If your volume is low, it becomes easy not to hear you. You can then become invisible and easy to ignore. People can speak and literally no one hears them. A soft-spoken man made a suggestion in a meeting which was overlooked, yet twenty minutes later another participant made almost the same suggestion. He spoke loudly. His suggestion was taken.

200. Pay attention to your rate. If people are always interrupting you, you may be speaking too slowly. If people keep saying, "whoa, wait a minute," chances are that you are speaking too quickly.

201. Don't giggle. Giggling is often heard at the end of people's sentences or statements. It's a habit that can make you appear nervous, insecure or childish. Both men and women do it and often don't know that they have this annoying mannerism and it can have consequences for the person. Jack was the expert. No one else in his department had the same grasp on e-commerce issues as he did. Yet, Jack was passed over a second time for a promotion. Finally, his manager told him that until he got rid of his nervous giggle, he was not going anywhere in the company. He was stunned. He didn't even realize that he was doing that.

202. Get a realistic idea of how you sound. Use your voice mail system to listen to your messages before you send them. Redo them if necessary. Over time you will gain awareness of the sound of your voice. (Hearing yourself will also help you review your word choice.)

What You Say:

203. **Watch out for qualifying words.** These are extra words that are added to sentences that can make even the smartest person sound tentative and unsure. Words like "kinda," "sorta," "maybe," "perhaps." "I was kinda, in a way, somewhat sure the deal would close." (Well, were you or weren't you!)

204. **Don't say, "I think" when you actually know.** If you are asked, "What time is the meeting on Monday?" do you answer, "I think the meeting is at 3 P.M." or "The meeting is at 3 P.M.?" If you are unsure of the time, you can use "I think." But don't say, "I think" when you know.

205. **Don't use "I don't know" as extra words.** This is not saying, "I don't know" because you truly don't know something. This is using "I don't know" as a way to discount what you have just said. "I suggest we implement the original plan. It's affordable, I don't know..."

206. **Don't say, "I'm sorry" for no reason.** One sales representative said to her customer, "I am sorry to bother you today." If she's servicing his account, how is she bothering him? Another man apologized for not having data for the report when his department was not responsible for generating it.

207. **Don't use questions, instead of direct statements.** When you use a question, you seem to give the person a choice. If there really isn't any choice, why use a question? "Could you get the proposal to me by 3 P.M.?" or "I need the proposal by three P.M."

208. **Eliminate distracting filler words.** These are words like "okay," "alright," "um," and "like." They are distracting and people stop listening. If people are counting the number of okays in your speech, it is not okay—they're not hearing what you're saying.

209. **Watch out for jargon and buzz words.** Every profession has its jargon and buzz words. If you are speaking to a colleague, chances are he or she knows what you are talking about. If you are talking to someone from another profession or company they may not know. When in doubt, leave them out.

210. **Avoid sexist language.** Women are women in the workplace. They are not girls. Both men and women use that word. Don't. Some people use the word "ladies." "Ladies" is better than "girls," but generally the preferred term is "women".

211. **Don't use curse words.** You know what they are. They make you sound bad. Don't use them!

212. **Grammar counts.** Even the smartest person will sound not so smart if he or she says, "I don't got none." Make sure your grammar skills are up to par.

DICTION DILEMMAS

Your diction, how you pronounce words, can enhance your professional appearance or take away from it. And often people don't realize they are using poor diction because it becomes a verbal habit.

SAY	DON'T SAY
Because	Cuz
Sandwich	Samwich
Them	Dem
Did you	Didja
Should have	Shoulda
Give me	Gimme
Want to	Wanna
Ought to	Otta
Going to	Gonna
Have to	Gotta
Did you eat?	Jeet
You	Youse

~FOUR~

INCREASING YOUR
EMPLOYABILITY QUOTIENT

*Become the CEO of You * Handling Criticism * How to Ask for a Raise ***
*Time Management Musts * Take Care of Yourself * The Etiquette of Team*
*Work * Develop Your Leadership Skills * Suggestions for Resumes and*
*Cover Letters * Must-Have Interviewing Skills*

D ID YOUR FATHER or grandfather work for the same company
for forty years? Many of us have parents and grandparents
who grew up in the generation where every hard-working person
was practically guaranteed lifetime employment.

Has the world changed! We all know that the world of lifetime
employment has just about disappeared. And this trend cuts both
ways. We've all heard about downsizing and lay-offs, but it isn't just
employers who don't have the same brand of loyalty to employees
that they used to. With the dotcom trend sweeping the globe, vol-
untary turnover in the workplace has reached huge proportions. The
average employee changes jobs every 3–4 years. And recent college
graduates can average a job change every fifteen months. It seems
like everyone is looking to be a part of the next big opportunity.

In this kind of low-stability job market there are two big questions: How do you achieve job security in your current position? And how do you get to take advantage of the next big career opportunity?

The answer is the same for both questions—you have to develop your Employability Quotient (EQ). Your EQ consists of all the little things you need to pay attention to to have both job security and also exciting career opportunities—everything from your on-the-job attitude to your time management skills and how you handle criticism.

If you come to work on time every day and never call in sick that means you have some good work habits, but it doesn't necessarily mean you have a high EQ. You have to pay attention to a range of details. Today's professionals who do pay attention to their EQs are the ones who look at creating job security and opportunities as part of their jobs. These are professionals who take an active, enthusiastic role in their career development. They may not be the CEO of their companies—yet! But they are, in effect, the CEOs of their own careers.

A high EQ means that no matter what the trend, you have taken charge of your career. EQ means that you do the best job you can for your employer and you know your skills, you know your profession, you know what you want and how to go about achieving it. EQ means you don't change jobs just because everyone is doing it; but you do take advantage of opportunities because you understand what the benefits can be to you and your career.

Become the CEO of You

213. **Be positive.** It may sound like a no-brainer, but if you expect the best, anticipate the best, you are more likely to get the best. Visualize yourself achieving career

success. Since we were kids, a friend of mine always saw himself making movies. He now makes Hollywood films for a living!

214. **Set goals.** In my experience, successful people are often goal-setters. You should be able to answer this question: Where do you want to be career-wise in six months? One year? Five years? Some people work towards financial goals, others work toward goals of position or knowledge. The point is to work toward something. Make sure your goals are realistic and that you periodically reevaluate and readjust them.

215. **Continue learning.** Most large organizations offer on- and off-site learning opportunities to broaden your skills and knowledge. Even if you're super busy, take time to take advantage of the training—your career advancement or your continued employability may depend upon acquiring new skills. If you work for a smaller company that doesn't offer learning programs, contact your professional association and find out who does offer seminars and lectures pertinent to your field. Many companies will reimburse you the cost.

216. **Consider continuing your formal education.** Most large and mid-size corporations do offer tuition reimbursement. Colleges and universities now offer incredibly flexible programs. You can earn a bachelor's or master's by attending classes at night, on weekends or via correspondence or online.

217. **Be proactive.** If you see an area of yourself that needs improvement or a situation that needs to be corrected, take action. Peter, a manager at a large manufacturing company, knew that his inability to make presentations was limiting his ability to advance. Yet he was afraid to

get up in front of a group. He finally talked himself into taking a presentation skills class and overcame his fear.

218. **Stay up to date with technology.** Yes, it changes fast but the people who make an effort to keep up with it are the ones who make themselves valuable to their organizations.

219. **Learn the politics of your organization.** You don't have to play "the game," but you want to know what is going on. Know your organization's promotion process. Are jobs posted? Does your boss have to recommend you? Do you have to talk to human resources? If you're not sure, find out.

220. **Find role models.** Role models are people you know personally or only by reputation. You learn from them by interacting with them or watching or reading about them. Identify areas that you want to develop and find people who do or have done that. Dr. Mae C. Jemison, the first African American woman astronaut, said her role model was Lt. Uhura from *Star Trek*. My role model was my former boss Ann Davis. She was one of the two highest women in an aerospace company when there were very few women in the field. I learned so much by watching her handle difficult situations with poise and grace!

221. **Find a mentor.** Find a person who is in a position that you aspire to be in or with qualities and skills you would like to emulate. The difference between a mentor and a role model is that a mentor takes an active role in your career development. Make a point to get together with your mentor on a regular basis. Actively learn from him or her. In my former career as a photographer, my mentor was Jon Falk. He was head photographer

at the *Philadelphia Bulletin,* one of the ten largest newspapers in this country at one time. His wife and I taught school and I looked to him as a resource as I was learning my skills. When I was trying out for my first full-time photographic job, I was assigned to shoot a football game. I didn't even understand the game, let alone know how to shoot it. Jon spent hours with me explaining the game and the best way to photograph it. I got the job. I never would have made it without him.

FIVE EASY WAYS TO FIND A MENTOR

Sign up. Many organizations, companies and professional associations recognize that mentoring is a powerful development tool and have instituted formal mentoring programs.

Ask someone. Most people will be flattered. Clare told me that she walked right up to an executive vice president in her organization whom she admired and simply asked, "Will you mentor me?" He said yes. They established a formal mentoring relationship with monthly meetings and telephone calls. Sometimes, he would set an agenda for their talks by suggesting books or articles for her to read and then they would discuss them. Other times, they would discuss any items that came up during their conversation. Clare has benefited greatly from his experience and wisdom.

Develop the relationship. The opposite of a formal mentoring connection is when a relationship develops over time usually with less structure. This can happen when you interact with someone, you ask him or her questions, solicit advice, follow their suggestions, and over time an informal mentoring relationship can develop. This was the way my relationship with Jon Falk developed.

Hire one. Many years ago, as I was developing my business, I had a paid marketing mentor, Joe Roy. He charged an hourly rate and I would call him monthly and pick his brain on how to best market my company. His expert advice and skills proved valuable to me. I still call him occasionally.

Network. Networking allows you to meet people in your profession. Join your professional association and organizations. (See pages 20-24 to learn the benefits and techniques of networking.)

222. **Become an enthusiastic expert.** An administrative assistant of a small manufacturing company had a knack for anything to do with computers. When her company got a new computer system, the other employees looked to her for help and she gave it—very willingly. She eventually asked her boss for additional company-paid training, had her job description expanded, and got a raise. Others in your organization will look to you if you're an expert in a particular area.

223. **Apply your expertise.** Once you've developed an area of expertise, put it to work. Offer to make presentations, give keynote speeches, and submit articles and opinion pieces to your professional trade magazines.

224. **Stay abreast of trends in your field.** Go to trade shows. Talk to your colleagues. Journals and newsletters in your field can keep you informed about what's happening in your field. Read them regularly.

225. **Be a wise risk-taker.** Ask yourself these questions before making a career move: 1. What's the worst that can happen? 2. What's the best that can happen? 3.

What's the risk of not taking the risk? If you know the answers to these questions, you will know whether to take the risk or not. My friend Milton left a secure job for an opportunity with a new dotcom venture. The company eventually failed but as Milton told me, "If it had been successful, I never would have forgiven myself for not taking the chance. And the skills I learned benefited me in my next job."

226. **Speak well of yourself.** Don't put yourself down and don't use self-deprecating humor. Why make yourself look bad?

227. **Accept compliments.** It's frustrating to try to compliment a person who won't accept it! Refusing a compliment is not gracious, it's silly and makes you look unprofessional. One boss said to his employee. "I am never going to compliment you again. You always negate them!" If someone compliments you thank him or her. If other people deserve recognition too, mention them, but don't deny yourself the recognition.

228. **Make sure your accomplishments are recognized.** If you want a high EQ, it's not enough to do good things—you must get recognition for doing them. You don't want to become obnoxious or a shameless self-promoter, but it's important to speak well of yourself and to let others know about your good work.

229. **Keep your work area neat and clean.** At least try to! A manager once told me that he won't promote people with sloppy work areas because to him, it's a sign of a disorganized, distracted mind. Whether or not he's right, there is a perception that you are disorganized if you work with piles of paper and files all around you. And it's true for me; I always feel better about myself and my work when my desk is organized.

230. **Evaluate your current position.** On a piece of paper, write down the strengths and drawbacks of your current position. Are you challenged? Are you getting benefits from the job? Does your boss support you? How could your job be better? Look at the list, evaluate the items, and if you can, take the steps necessary to correct the drawbacks.

231. **Decide if it is time to move on.** Why stay in a job that makes you miserable unless you are certain it will change, the benefits outweigh the drawbacks or you will be promoted out of it? It's hard to work hard effectively when you're unhappy.

232. **Stay challenged.** Boredom saps your energy and often promotes negative thinking. If your job has gotten dull and predictable, ask your boss or supervisor for new responsibility. Volunteer for a department project. Join a cross-departmental team.

233. **Put your ideas "out there."** Do you sit in the monthly marketing meeting and think of ideas but keep them to yourself because you're not sure how others will react to them? Well why not take a risk? Your suggestions may in fact be excellent and will get you noticed. Here's a tip: Prepare ahead of time. Think of the meeting agenda and where your input may be needed. Think how you will express your ideas. The topic may not come up, but at least you are prepared if it does.

234. **Ask for feedback.** If you want to get ahead, but feel you're not moving ahead, ask your boss or supervisor for feedback. What can I be doing better? How can I get the plum assignments? The feedback you get may surprise you. Kevin, an account executive for a PR firm, was upset that he never got assigned to any of the highly visible department projects. Finally, he asked his

boss why he wasn't chosen. His boss was surprised that Kevin had any interest in these projects. He thought Kevin wasn't interested in taking on jobs that required overnight travel.

Handling Criticism

"My former manager would always cry whenever she got criticized. The higher-ups discounted her as a result. She never went anywhere in the company and finally left."

235. **If you ask for feedback, you may end up hearing some criticism.** A critical employability skill is learning how to handle feedback with good grace and humor. The following five points will help you:

236. **Don't get defensive.** If you're hearing unpleasant criticism and you're feeling upset, stay calm. Don't offer heated rebuttals to everything you're being told. Just listen, breathe deeply. You can explain that you would like some time to consider the feedback and you would like to discuss it later.

237. **Don't react with tears, either.** It's not professional. If it happens, force yourself to continue talking or excuse yourself for a moment, go to the restroom, get yourself together and then go back into the meeting.

238. **Be open-minded.** You may not like hearing what your boss has to say, but you may need to hear it. Though initially unpleasant, getting feedback may help you raise your employability quotient and eventually help you get promoted.

239. **Ask for specific examples.** Clara was confused by the feedback that her boss gave her—that she was too negative. She asked for specific examples. He told her, "You routinely show up late for the weekly meeting and you roll your eyes at other people in the department."

240. **Be willing to change.** If you've received valid feedback, seriously consider changing your behavior. Clara's initial response to the negative attitude comment was "No, I don't!" But after mature reflection, she had to admit that her attitude could be taken as negative. She made a conscious effort to change.

241. **Consider the criticizer.** You may be getting negative feedback from someone who has an ax to grind. If this is the truly the case, it is usually best to put the experience behind you and move on. If you are getting feedback from an expert, consider the feedback a gift and consider the comments carefully. If you feel that your boss is treating you unfairly, you may have to adapt your behavior anyway— he or she is the boss. If the negative feedback is a way of life, consider your options. It may be time to move on.

How to Ask for a Raise

"I kept thinking my boss would get the hint that I was due a raise. Unfortunately, he didn't and by the time I said something, I had lost five months."

You may believe that you deserve to make more money, yet that doesn't mean asking for it is going to be easy. In fact, asking your boss for a raise is one of the most nerve-wracking and difficult conversations you may ever have at work.

Only you can make the decision about whether or not you should ask for a raise, keep your mouth shut or look for a new job. But if you decide that you want to talk to your boss about your salary, how do you approach this difficult conversation? Though there isn't any magic formula for guaranteeing a raise, if you follow these guidelines you can increase your chances that your conversation will be a positive one.

242. **Prepare what you are going to say.** Don't have an important conversation such as this on the spur of the moment without preparing. You will be acting out of emotion, which can be detrimental. When you're prepared you're able to be calm and focused.

243. **Get as much information as you can about what others in your field are making.** Most trade publications publish periodic salary issues where you can get this information. Your industry association may also have this information.

244. **Prove your worth.** Explain what you have accomplished, how you have saved the company money, increased sales, enhanced morale, improved productivity, etc.

245. **Don't make negative comparisons.** "Joe makes more money than I do and I work twice as hard." Your boss may disagree that you do more work than Joe does.

246. **Ask for the raise.** "My work load has increased significantly now that I'm handling the key accounts. I would like my salary increased to reflect that."

247. **Don't make demands or issue threats.** "If you don't give me a raise, I'm quitting." If you do give an ultimatum, even one that's nicely worded, it could backfire on you. "I love my job but I won't be able to stay here

unless you pay me more." If they won't pay you more, you will then have to find another job.

248. **If you get turned down, ask why.** Is it your work, policy or lack of funds? Knowing the reason will help you evaluate your options. Ask yourself: Is it time to move on? I know a computer programmer who was certain he was going to get the raise he thought he deserved. When he didn't, he was crushed. Eventually though, it motivated him to look for a new, better-paying job.

Time Management Musts

"I kept avoiding getting a planner. I wasn't going to be one of those phony people who had to check his planner to do lunch! I finally got one as a gift and I can't believe how much more productive I am."

249. **Plan.** In today's fast-pace world, if you don't manage your time, it will manage you. Do you just keep all your "to dos" in your head? Are you one of those people who ends up with your desk and computer covered with Post-It-Notes? If so, consider using a daily planning sheet or one main "to do" list instead. One master list will help keep you focused. Many people have easy-to-use daily planners that go unused on their computers. Or Palm Pilots can help a lot. Take a few minutes and learn how to use these time-organizing devices.

250. **Prioritize your activities.** Every day, decide what is most important to accomplish. Try to stay focused on

that task until it is finished. Then move on to the next thing.

251. **Set realistic deadlines.** A systems analyst told me that everything takes him three days longer than he thinks it will and that he worries it makes him look bad to his boss. I suggested that he simply add three days to any deadline he sets and then firmly try to meet that deadline.

252. **Transform waiting time into accomplishment.** I never go anywhere without a speech or talk to edit, a book to read or e-mail I've printed out from my computer. That way, if I have an appointment and have to wait, I can still get work done. This makes waiting time more productive and me less stressed out.

253. **Delegate.** What do you have to do and what can be done by others? Many people don't delegate because they fear that others won't be able to do the work. They therefore end up with too much work to do and not enough time to do it in. If you try to do everything yourself, you will often fail. Work with others, train them, assist them, you will be amazed at how much time you will gain!

Take Care of Yourself

"I was working extra hard on a big, high-visibility project. My wife kept telling me that I wasn't taking care of myself, especially that I wasn't eating right or exercising. I kept saying, 'I'll take care of myself when this project is over.' One day I was sitting in a meeting and got squeezing pains in my chest. I thought I was having a heart attack. I was rushed to the hospital. The doctors told

me the attack was stress related. It was embarrassing more than anything else. I started taking better care of myself the next day."

254. **Exercise.** I have met and worked with some of the busiest—and most successful—executives in corporate America and guess what? Many of them manage to exercise on a regular basis. It's critical that you exercise regularly to control your stress and maintain health. Take advantage of company gyms and lunchtime aerobics. Even a brisk walk at lunch can do the trick.

255. **Stop during your hectic day to breathe.** Most of us get so busy and stressed out during our workday that we literally forget to breathe properly. Those shallow breaths we take help keep us stressed out. Stop what you're doing and take a deep breath through your nose. Breathe so you expand your entire lower then upper body. Then release it slowly to the count of seven. Do this three or four times and you'll feel relaxed and reenergized.

256. **Schedule down time for yourself.** Even if you can work 24/7 don't! You will burn out. Make sure you have regular activities that you enjoy that don't have anything to do with work. Read a novel, take an art class, play with your kids.

257. **Get enough sleep.** You can't concentrate or focus your energies on work if you're too tired to keep your eyes open.

258. **Eat a healthy diet.** I know, I know, it's so hard to eat well, but you will feel better and work better if you do. Make sure to eat breakfast, it will help you focus and work well early in the morning. Avoid sugary snacks for pick-me-ups. They don't work. Snacks containing both protein and carbs will keep you going throughout the day.

The Etiquette of Team Work

"One of our team members routinely drops the ball when we have dinner programs for our customers. He doesn't keep track of the customers that RSVP to him and then calls at the last minute saying he cannot attend. I don't want to work with him anymore!"

259. **Understand the goal of the team.** If you don't understand the purpose, then you can't work to fulfill it. If you're not sure, then ask someone to clarify it for you.

260. **Work hard.** One of the biggest complaints I get from team members is that the others on the team don't do their job. You don't want to get a reputation as the person who doesn't do his or her share. Do your best work, even if others aren't.

261. **Don't procrastinate.** Team deadlines should be upheld as closely as you uphold personal deadlines. If you tell a team member that something will be done by a certain deadline, meet your deadline.

262. **Help others.** You're all working towards the same goal, so if you can help someone out, do so. The next go around, you may be the one that needs help!

263. **Make sure your talents and expertise are fully utilized.** If you're suited for a particular assignment and don't get it, don't be shy, speak up. The other team members may not know what your talents are.

264. **Be a full participant.** Attend and participate in meetings, team activities and social events.

265. **Be current and up to date.** Know any new procedures, guidelines, and company policies that effect the running of the group.

266. Be honest with your team members. If you have a problem or personality conflict with another team member, confront that person honestly and directly. Don't let the problem fester and don't complain to other team members.

267. Share the spotlight. If you're working on a team and get personally recognized for your efforts, make sure to include your other team members in the praise and recognition.

Develop Your Leadership Skills

"I was new to the company. Yet, I quickly figured out that it wasn't my manager who was leading us, it was one of my co-workers. He was the one that others in the department looked to for guidance. He wasn't officially in charge, but he was our leader. I made a point to work closely with him. I learned a lot from him."

WHAT THE LEADERS HAVE TO SAY ABOUT LEADERSHIP...

"You need integrity, intelligence and energy to succeed. Integrity is totally a matter of choice—and it is habit-forming."
—Warren Buffett, CEO of Berkshire-Hathaway

"You have no right to be a leader if you don't have it in your soul to build others."
—Jack Welch, CEO, General Electric

"Being a decision maker...the ability to make a decision, even if it's a wrong one, can't be underestimated."
—Darla Moore, president of the private investment firm Rainwater Inc., named to Fortune's 1999 list of the 50 most powerful women

"The very essence of leadership is that you have to have a vision. It's got to be a vision you articulate clearly and forcefully on every occasion."
—Theodore Hessburgh, president of the University of Notre Dame

268. **Identify the leaders in your own organization.** We are not all destined to be leaders. Yet we all can learn from leaders and benefit from knowing the key qualities that leaders have and using them to enhance our own careers. Besides the CEO or president of your company, who are the key players who others turn to for help and inspiration? Watch these people and see how they interact with others. Consider asking someone with leadership skills to become your mentor.

269. **Read books on leadership and/or biographies about great leaders.** Many of today's great business leaders and visionaries write books or are written about. Find out what makes them tick.

270. **Be a motivator.** Leaders inspire others into action. But you can't do that until you are highly motivated yourself. Once you're motivated, think about how you can become a motivating force to others around you. Whether it's getting others in your department to join the company softball team or overseeing the launch of a

new product or service, motivating others is vital to your career success and the well being of any organization.

271. **Treat others with courtesy and respect.** Though there are exceptions, most people who are successful leaders are people who treat others well. The managing partner of a law firm said that on a final exam in law school, the last question was: "What is the name of the person who empties the trash cans?" He said he didn't know but that it made him realize how important it was to know.

272. **Mentor others.** What better way to practice your leadership skills?

273. **Demonstrate that you are a problem-solver.** Don't just get your work done, solve problems. They don't have to be huge problems to make an impact. Take the initiative—make suggestions on how things could run more smoothly in your department.

274. **Learn to accept responsibility.** If the numbers in the report were wrong admit it. Don't cast blame. Leaders are people who take responsibility for their actions, even when doing so is difficult. A team of software developers were involved in a difficult meeting in which they had to admit to the marketing director that their latest product wasn't panning out. Excuses were offered and blame was cast. Finally, one brave developer said, "Looking back now, we've learned some valuable lessons…" and he proceeded to state what went wrong, why, and how it could be prevented in the future. He was chosen to head the next product development team.

275. **Think creatively.** Leaders are known for coming up with the inspired solutions and innovative ideas. Start flexing your creative muscle no matter what you're

working on. Find a better or different way to do something you've done a hundred times. Exploring your creative outlets outside of work will encourage you to think more creatively at work.

276. **Volunteer to lead others.** If you want to lead others, but don't have any experience, ask to head a project or team. If you don't have any opportunities within your organization, look outside of it. Is there a non-profit committee or a board that would give you the opportunity to lead? Any leadership experience will be valuable. One CEO told me that everything he learned about leadership he learned by coaching his nine-year-old son's soccer team. Not only did he learn from the game but also improved his diplomacy and interpersonal skills by interacting with the children's parents!

SUGGESTIONS FOR RESUMES AND COVER LETTERS

"A friend called to say that his company had an immediate and urgent opening for someone with my skills and background. He knew I was unsatisfied with my current position and asked me to e-mail him my resume ASAP. I couldn't because my resume wasn't up-to-date. My girlfriend who helped me with my last one was away on a business trip and my resume was on her computer. By the time I redid my resume, the job was filled."

Keep your resume up to date. I'm always amazed at the number of people who say they are looking for a new career opportunity and yet when I ask to see their resume, they admit they don't have a current one ready and waiting. "Then you're not seriously looking," I tell them. In today's job market, you need to be prepared to act quickly.

Get professional help for your resume. If you're not the world's best resume writer, why not find and hire someone who is?

Keep your resume simple. Hiring managers and recruiters tell me that you don't need a four-page resume to be impressive. In fact, you may be more impressive if you can show your stuff on a one-to one-and-a-half-page resume.

Don't lie.

If you are sending your resume electronically, know the correct format to use. Also be aware that if you are posting your resume on an electronic bulletin board or website, others may see it—including your boss or co-workers.

Target the cover letter to the specific job. While your resume is a look at your general career history and accomplishments, a cover letter is your opportunity to list or elaborate upon specific achievements, talents and contributions as they apply to specific jobs you're applying for. But keep it brief—this isn't the place to give your full history.

Use the proper salutation. Always err on the side of formality. Dear Mr. O'Brien or Dear Ms. Bradshaw. If you don't have a name, use a non-gender specific term such as Dear Recruiter or Dear Company Representative. Recruiters have told me they have thrown away letters that started "Dear Sir."

Convey confidence. You don't want to be a braggart, but if you're not going to write well of yourself, who will? You always want to be honest and direct but you should be confident and enthusiastic as well. "As my references will tell you, I'm an extremely hard working person. I take pride in my work..."

Make both your resume and cover letter perfect. No typos or errors. A clean layout and readable design. Hiring managers look at them as an indication of your writing and communication skills. And whether or not you pay attention to the details.

Use a good quality bond paper in a neutral color. The envelope should match as well.

Must-Have Interviewing Skills

"I kept losing jobs because I didn't know how to interview. I would get nervous and either clam up during interviews or talk too much. I finally went to a career coach and we practiced interviewing. What a difference! I got the next job I interviewed for."

277. **Remember that it is your resume that will get you the interview but your interviewing skills will get you the job!**

278. **Do your homework.** If you're seeking a new position within your company, find out as much as you can about the department from others. If it's a new company, request catalogs, brochures, or an annual report—if one is available. Go to the library or search the Internet for articles or news about the company.

279. **Wear the right clothing.** Your clothing should reflect the business climate and position for which you're interviewing.

Generally, a suit is appropriate. I once interviewed for a job in southern California and when the manager offered me the job he commented that he was impressed that I looked so professional in my suit. Dotcom recruiters tell me that they recommend that people interview in suits though chances are they won't wear them on the job. Remember to shine your shoes. Carry a high-quality briefcase or handbag. Double check your grooming.

280. **Practice.** Some interviewers begin by asking you about yourself or want to know why you want to leave your present position. Think your answers through ahead of time and be ready to offer a brief verbal introduction to your resume. You want to focus on the areas of your expertise that pertain to the job for which you're interviewing. If possible, ask a friend to play the role of the interviewer with you.

281. **Prepare your references.** You should have the names and telephone numbers of references, or letters of reference, ready to offer.

282. **During the interview, the key is to make sure your image says "professional."**

283. **Be on time.** Leave yourself enough time in case you have problems with directions or finding parking. You also want to have enough time to use the restroom and check your appearance one last time.

284. **Shake hands, both at the beginning and at the end of the interview.** Many hiring managers tell me they are impressed when job applicants do this. Generally, even if the interviewer doesn't offer his or her hand, you should. Make sure your grip is firm and confident. Don't forget to smile and make eye contact.

285. **Wait to be seated.** If the interviewer doesn't offer you a seat, ask where you should sit.

286. **Appear confident.** Be aware of your posture throughout the interview. Sit up straight and tall in your chair. Maintain eye contact. Don't fidget or play with things or touch anything on the interviewer's desk.

287. **Emphasize your strengths and abilities.** Tell the interviewer exactly why you're the best candidate for the position.

288. **Keep your answers brief and to the point.** Stay focused. Don't ramble off on tangents. Answer questions in a straightforward, pleasant manner. Smile and occasionally use the interviewer's name.

289. **No matter what the interviewer asks you, keep your cool.** Don't show annoyance or allow yourself to become exasperated. If the question is inappropriate, and you truly don't want to answer it, you can always calmly and politely ask the interviewer how your answer would pertain to the position.

290. **Get immediate feedback.** Sometimes simply asking a question can give you valuable information as to whether or not you will be seriously considered for the job. For example, "Based on our discussions, how do you see my skills fitting in with the job we just discussed?"

291. **Ask for the job.** It isn't impolite to do this, but it's essential to be polite when doing it. You can say, "I'm very interested in this position because..." and state your reasons why.

292. **Establish the next step.** Ask the interviewer when he or she expects to make a decision and when you can

expect to be contacted. Once you have that information, end on a positive note. Even if you decide the position isn't what you want, smile, shake hands, and thank the interviewer pleasantly.

293. **Follow up.** Send a thank-you letter immediately. State your interest in the position and reemphasize some of the main reasons why you're qualified for the job. Even if you're not interested in the job, send a note thanking the interviewer for his or her time.

294. **If you don't get the position, try to find out why.** You may not want to be criticized, but it may be of great value in preparing for future interviews.

∼ FIVE ∼

SUCCESSFUL SOCIALIZING

*Blunder-Free Business Dining * Ordering in for a Working Lunch * Eating
in the Cafeteria * Buffet Dining Guidelines * The Etiquette of Dining Solo*
Six Frequently Asked Questions About Business Dining * Liquor
Guidelines* Office Party Perfection*

H OW YOU HANDLE yourself at a business-related social function
matters. Whether it's a lunch with co-workers, a formal business dinner where you're hosting clients, or the good old office
holiday party, you will be judged by your behavior.

If you're at a lunch meeting, your potential employers, customers
or upper management aren't just looking to see that you don't slop
soup on the table. They're often looking for self-assurance, social
finesse—and you guessed it—that you're paying attention to a wide
variety of details. Let's be honest and realistic; if you can't handle the
little things at lunch or dinner, why should anyone think you could
handle the big things, like the big account or the bigger job?

Most of the little things featured in this section have to do with
business dining. That's because when we socialize with our
co-workers or clients we most often do so around food and drink.

There are also a great number of people out there in the wide world of work, otherwise smart, confident, savvy professionals, who get the jitters about business dining. They're afraid of making a mistake. And the reality is that there is no shortage of opportunity for error when dining with other people.

I once received an urgent telephone call from an HR executive of one of today's most highly regarded financial services corporations. She wanted me to come in and immediately teach my business dining seminars. I soon discovered that one of the organization's biggest customers was lost due to a business-dining blunder. A director had licked his knife in front of an important client at a business dinner. The client was so thoroughly put off by this behavior that he took his multi-million dollar business elsewhere. You would think that the director would know better than to lick his knife, getting as far in his business life as he had. But he didn't, and it was a costly mistake.

People, often unknowingly, make all kinds of business-dining blunders. Do you think people who chew with their mouths open are purposely trying to be offensive? No, they just don't realize they have that bad habit. Ignorance is no excuse, however, and it won't get you off the hook if you hang yourself on one by making a mistake at a business meal.

But if you learn the rules, the finer points of business dining, if you pay attention to the little things you will feel more confident and self-assured when you're socializing for business. If you're worried or distracted about which bread plate is yours or how in the world to get an escargot out of that little shell then you can't focus on making an outstanding impression with your technical knowledge and your professional behavior.

Blunder-Free Business Dining

"We were down to our last two candidates for the job. At the lunch interview, one of them treated the server rudely. He acted like our waiter was beneath him. I was very turned off by his behavior and the other person got the job."

295. **Understand the point of the business meal.** You dine to conduct business and establish relationships. You may need to eat, but you are not there for the food.

296. **Get to know a couple of good restaurants.** Know that the food and atmosphere of the place is appropriate for business. Go there when entertaining.

297. **Take charge.** If you are the host, you need to be in charge and manage all of the logistics of the meal. Make a reservation. If your client is a non-smoker, make sure your table is in the no-smoking section. Direct your guest to the most comfortable seat or the one with the best view.

298. **Put your napkin on your lap as soon as you are seated.** At a formal dinner, etiquette dictates that the hostess should do so first. Don't tuck your napkin into your shirt or belt. Remember, you're not at a family picnic!

299. **Use good posture at the table.** Don't slouch in your seat.

300. **Don't launch into business discussions right away.** Make small talk first. In general, the time to discuss business matters is after the meal has been ordered.

301. **Treat your server courteously.** Do not call your server "Honey," "Boy," "Girl," "Sweetie," "Garcon," or anything else that may be offensive.

302. **Know which bread plate or water glass is yours.** Here's a trick for remembering which one is yours: "Food" has four letters and "left" has four letters. Bread is food, so your bread plate is on the left. "Drink" has five letters and so does "right." Your water glass is on the right.

303. **The host should make recommendations on items to order such as "The chicken here is excellent."**

304. **Make your selection by the time everyone else is ready to order.** Don't ask the waiter to explain everything on the menu. You'll seem indecisive and you'll be annoying. If you're the host, make sure your guest's order is taken first, regardless of gender. (See Gender Etiquette Essentials, Section 2 for suggestions for women.)

305. **If you don't how to eat something, don't order it.** If you don't know what it is, don't order it! It's okay to ask a question or two, but don't overdo it.

306. **Don't order messy meals.** Remember that the point of the meal isn't to eat your favorite foods. It's business; so don't even think about that big, juicy hamburger! Spaghetti, lobster, and French onion soup with lots of cheese on top are also bad choices. They have "splash" or "mess" potential. Order what you know will be easy to eat.

307. **Don't make negative comments about the restaurant or the food.** Unless your food is inedible don't send it back.

308. **Don't lick your utensils or fingers.** People do this all the time without realizing it!

309. **Do not make noise when you eat.** No slurping or lip smacking.

310. **Know the types of utensils.** The largest fork is generally the entrée fork. The salad fork is smaller. The largest spoon is usually the soup spoon.

311. **As a general rule of thumb, navigate your place setting from the outside in.**

312. **Use your utensils properly.** I am amazed at how many people hold their fork like a pitchfork! People notice. A manager told her fiancé that she was not taking him to any more company dinners until he learned to use his utensils properly. She was embarrassed.

313. **Either the American or Continental style for handling utensils is acceptable in the U.S.** Be consistent and correct in your use. **American:** Hold the knife in your right hand and the fork in your left, tines down. Cut up to three pieces of meat. Put the knife down on your plate and switch the fork to your right hand, tines up. **Continental:** Same starting and cutting procedure except don't switch your fork to the other hand. Bring the fork to your mouth tines down. The knife remains in the right hand and can be used to put food onto the back of the fork.

314. **When you're finished eating place your utensils in the finished position.** If the dinner plate is a clock, your fork and knife are placed in parallel lines at approximately 10 and 4 o'clock. Knife on top, handles towards the four.

315. **No grooming at the table.** Don't reapply your lipstick or comb your hair at the table. Don't use the napkin as a tissue. Never use your hand to clear crumbs off the table.

316. **Don't fight over the bill.** The host is the person who does the inviting, and that person pays the bill—regardless of gender. (See gender etiquette essentials, page 43 for more information)

317. **Leave an appropriate tip.** Generally you will leave between 15–20 percent for a gratuity. I know a VP who hates when one of the managers underneath her picks up the tab because she's known as a cheap tipper. As the guest don't argue or try to leave the tip.

318. **Thank the host.** Thank your host for the meal immediately after and send a handwritten thank you note within twenty-four hours if you were the guest at the meal.

ORDERING IN FOR A WORKING LUNCH:

319. **Be prepared.** Make sure you have the proper utensils, napkins, and plates on hand if you're ordering in or lunching through a meeting.

320. **Don't assume that you know what everyone wants and likes to eat.** If you're ordering, ask people what they want or order a variety of sandwiches or salads. You want to ensure that everyone will have something they can and want to eat.

321. **Don't order messy meals.** A man told me that during a working lunch he ordered a cheesesteak while his colleagues all ordered simple cold sandwiches. He said he took one bite and he regretted it. His sandwich was very sloppy and he had to move all of his papers off of

the conference table for fear that they would become soiled. It interfered with his ability to work.

322. **Don't talk with your mouth full.** When you're having a working lunch, it's tempting to talk and chew. Make sure you have swallowed before you start talking.

EATING IN THE CAFETERIA:

323. **Pay attention to your table manners.** Even though it's a more casual environment, all your table manners still apply. It matters how you behave!

324. **Make up your mind while you're in line.** Don't wait until it's your turn to order. The people behind you will resent the hold-up.

325. **Don't comment on the food while standing in line.** You may be tempted to make a comment since you usually can see the food. But don't. Unless the comments are positive, keep them to yourself. People don't want to hear negative comments about food that they are choosing.

326. **Don't groom.** Again, just because it's a less formal environment, you don't have license to comb your hair or apply lipstick. I was in a large corporate cafeteria and a woman was polishing her nails at a nearby table!

BUFFET DINING GUIDELINES:

327. **You can make as many trips to the buffet as necessary, but don't overdo it!** You don't want it to interfere with the conversation. Remember that you are there for business, not the food.

328. **Do not overfill your plate.** It's messy if you do. And choose foods that go well together.

329. **Eat foods in a typical order—appetizer, soup, entrée, dessert.** You don't get everything at once. If you did, your place setting and the table would be crowded.

330. **Take a new, clean plate every time you return to the buffet line.** The waiter is to remove your used plate.

THE ETIQUETTE OF DINING SOLO:

331. **Don't be embarrassed that you're eating alone.** You are not a second-class citizen—you're a paying customer. You do not need to sit at the bar to eat, though you can if you're more comfortable eating there. If you are seated at a table in a bad location, you can say, "I'd like a seat a little farther from the door," or "I'll wait at the bar until you have another table."

332. **Remember that you are sharing the space with strangers.** It can be tempting to eavesdrop, but don't, or at least be discreet. Don't interrupt other people's conversations, though at times it may be appropriate to make a comment if you have made eye contact. If the other people do not continue the conversation, do not continue to talk.

333. **The restaurant is not an extension of your office.** You can read a book while you're waiting for your meal to arrive, but don't fumble with lots of papers or make a lot of noise. Your cell phone should not ring. It's disturbing to others. You don't want to set up a laptop. It generally takes up too much space and if you spill something, you can ruin your computer.

334. Your table manners always matter. While eating, you don't
want to be an eyesore or a distraction to someone else.

SIX FREQUENTLY ASKED QUESTIONS ABOUT BUSINESS DINING

Through my website and e-mail, and during my seminars, people
ask me all kinds of business etiquette–related questions. Though
the topics vary and encompass a range of issues, I can always
count on a good number about business dining. It makes sense—
eating in front of others when you don't know the basics of etiquette can make you feel uncomfortable and unsure of yourself.
Dining mistakes can often lead to conflict and embarrassment.

Take, for example, the man who was out to dinner with his boss.
He started complaining quite bitterly about the lousy service they
were receiving. His boss asked him why he was getting upset
when he, in fact, was signaling the waiter that he was not ready to
order by keeping his menu open. "Close the menu and the waiter
will come over," she said. He responded, "Oh my gosh, for twenty
years I've been getting upset in restaurants because I haven't
known the signal!"

*Knowing the answer to these six commonly asked questions
will help you feel more at ease when eating with colleagues
or clients:*

Q: I know it's not OK to blow on your soup to cool it off, but can I put
ice cubes in it?
A: No. Just wait. It's usually not very long before the soup cools off.

Q: Is it OK to flip my tie over my shoulder while I eat?
A: No. Sit up properly and lean only slightly forward when eating and
you won't need to worry about your tie ending up in your food.

Q: I have been putting empty sugar packets back in the container after I use them. I know there must be a better place, but I don't know where.

A: Fold the empty packet and place it under your plate.

Q: If I don't drink and my customer orders one, what do I do?

A: Order an iced tea, sparkling water or a soda. You don't want your guest drinking alone.

Q: I like a lot of pepper, and the pepper shaker usually doesn't flow quickly enough for me. Can I take the top off to pour the pepper on my food?

A: No. Be patient and remember that good food is seasoned by the chef!

Q: Can I drink soda or beer from the bottle at a dinner?

A: No. Use a glass.

LIQUOR GUIDELINES:

335. **Stay sober.** Here's a general guideline: business and liquor don't mix! Drunk business people often behave unprofessionally, inappropriately and say and do things that come back to haunt them later. Even when casually dining or socializing with co-workers, be careful not to drink too much. You don't want to do or say something that you'll regret later.

336. **Set a limit for yourself and stick to it.** If you don't set a limit it is very easy to keep on drinking. You still have to work with these people on Monday. A smart limit for most of us is one drink.

337. **If your job interview is taking place over lunch or dinner, do not drink.** You may be judged poorly for drinking during the interview. If the person interviewing you orders a bottle of wine, it's usually best to let the wine be poured into your glass, but then drink very little.

338. **Do not order beer at a formal dinner.** Remember this is about business, not having your favorite drink. I was teaching a formal dining course to a Fortune 100 company. The director was drinking beer from the bottle as he mingled with his employees. He was the one who wanted to have the class because he thought his employees needed the information!

339. **Know a little about wine.** Wine is to complement the food. White wine is generally served with fish and white meat, red wine with red meat—but these are not binding rules. Popular reds include Cabernet Sauvignon, Zinfandel and Merlot; whites include Chardonnay, Pinot Grigio and Sauvignon Blanc. If you are unsure about ordering wine at a meal, take a class at an adult school or look up your questions at http://www.wine.wsj.com. This site is a great wine resource.

340. **As the host you are to order the wine.** You should ask your guests for input. If one of your guests is an expert on wines, you can ask that person to pick the wine. You can also ask the wine steward (sommelier) for suggestions.

341. **The wine steward serves the wine.** He or she brings the wine to the table and presents it to the host to make sure the correct wine will be served. After opening the bottle, the wine steward may offer the cork to the host. You check the cork for moistness to be sure it has been properly stored. After you have examined it, replace it on the table. A small amount of wine is poured into the

host's glass so he or she can taste the wine. The host nods approval and the wine is poured into the guests' glasses. The host's glass is filled last.

342. **Don't send the wine back to impress your guests.** Wine is sent back only if it is spoiled or flawed and not because you don't like the taste.

343. **The wine steward should refill the glasses.** The host may also do so. Do not fill the glass more than two-thirds full.

344. **Hold the glass correctly.** The wineglass is held by the stem. If you need to warm up the wine—if the white is too cold or the red needs to be a little warmer, you can cup the glass.

345. **Be responsible.** If your guest drinks too much, arrange transportation for that person.

OFFICE PARTY PERFECTION:

346. **Make sure you attend.** Attendance at the company holiday party isn't optional. Your absence will be noticed, and most likely, noted by your boss and other higher-ups. Make a point to be there on time. At a recent seminar a young woman asked me if she should go to the CEO's holiday party. She didn't want to give up her Saturday night out with friends. I had a simple answer: Go!

347. **Don't drink too much at your office holiday party!** As mentioned above, stay sober! Of all places the holiday party seems to be the easiest for people to lose control. We have all heard horror stories about employees who danced wildly or made inappropriate remarks. You

will be held responsible and there are consequences. A bank manager swears he got promoted because his boss got drunk and said such outrageous racist comments at the holiday party, she was fired.

348. **Watch your body language.** Don't let others know if you're bored. Even if the party is dull, it's bad manners to let others see how bored you are. Pay attention to your body language. Don't frown, slouch, or yawn. You also need to stay for an appropriate amount of time.

349. **Dress appropriately.** It may be a party but it's still business. Nothing too short, too low, or *too* anything.

350. **Prepare your spouse.** If you're attending a company holiday party with your spouse or significant other, prepare him or her in advance on appropriate dress and topics of conversation. Remember, his or her behavior will reflect on you. If you do not have a significant other, check with organizers if it is appropriate for you to bring a friend. If you attend with family members, make a point of introducing them to co-workers. Make sure your children are well behaved. And if your spouse is supposed to attend, make sure he or she does. A CEO told his vice president that he was not advancing any further in the company unless his wife started attending company functions.

351. **Don't forget that your behavior always matters.** Don't make major personal revelations. Don't gossip. Don't make the mistake of thinking that just because this is a party, you can address the company president by his or her first name. Try to get to know other people in your office that you don't normally get a chance to interact with.

352. **Send a thank-you note to the party's organizer.**

HANDLING TECHNOLOGY PROFESSIONALLY

*E-mail Etiquette for Everyone * Salutations and Closings * Telephone Etiquette * Smart Cellular Telephone Use * Voice Mail Essentials * Videoconferencing * Miscellaneous Techno-Etiquette*

THERE'S NOTHING LIKE a quick e-mail or voice mail to update your colleagues or to get information to a client quickly. Using today's business technology to communicate is fast, efficient and inexpensive.

Yet, these wonderfully convenient forms of communication can also be annoying, rude and a source of office conflict. If you want to communicate successfully and send a positive message to others, including potential clients or customers, you need to pay attention to all the little things that make up your techno-etiquette expertise.

Even people who are normally not rude can make techno-etiquette mistakes. Sometimes big ones! I know a woman who was responding to an e-mail from her boss and was letting off steam about her latest assignment. She had no intention of sending it until she had gotten rid of the foul language. She accidentally sent it before she was done!

A dotcom manager was reprimanded for programming his Palm Pilot in a meeting. He told me he worked for a technology company so he figured it was okay. It wasn't. He'll never make that kind of mistake again.

People are surprised that in addition to cell phones and e-mail, I include guidelines for using the good old telephone. The reason I do is simple—people are still making mistakes using our oldest business technology.

E-mail Etiquette for Everyone

"I was working on landing a new account. The manager I was dealing with told me to get him the quote overnight. He works for a pretty high-tech company and his e-mail was listed on his business card, so I figured I would send it via e-mail. When I called to follow up, he said he never received it—he only checks his e-mail once a day so he must have missed it. He told me that he prefers to receive packages the old-fashioned way—by overnight mail. I just didn't think to ask at the time."

353. **Understand that the rules of writing apply.** Many people feel that because e-mail is more casual, it's okay to forget about grammar, spelling and typos. They're wrong. The quality of your writing always counts. The message, no matter how it's written or delivered, reveals something about you and the quality of your work.

354. **Learn how your system works.** And follow your company guidelines on appropriate use of e-mail.

355. **Don't contribute to e-mail overload.** Respect other people's "electronic space" by sending messages only when

necessary and only to the necessary people. Many people do not want to receive jokes or chain letters, either.

356. **Don't give out someone's e-mail address without permission.**

357. **Don't e-mail your new clients until you're sure that he or she is comfortable communicating that way.** Just because e-mail is second nature to you, that doesn't mean it's second nature to all. Just because an e-mail address is on someone's business card doesn't mean they really use it. A colleague of mine hates it when clients e-mail her. She wants to talk to them. She feels she can more effectively gauge their needs and moods and therefore service the account better.

358. **Check your e-mail regularly.** You don't want messages to pile up.

359. **Respond to e-mails within a reasonable amount of time.** A general business guideline is to respond within twenty-four hours. If the person has requested an immediate reply and you can't give one, let him or her know when you will able to get the information.

360. **Do not mark a message urgent, unless it really is.** You will get a reputation for crying electronic wolf.

361. **Never forward e-mail if you think or know the sender has intended it to be for your eyes only.**

362. **Use the "Out of Office Auto Reply" feature, if you have it.** It automatically e-mails the sender that you are out of the office. You can detail in the message when you will be returning and who to contact in case your correspondent needs immediate attention.

363. **Document your e-mail if necessary.** If you're sending time-sensitive materials, use the feature on your e-mail system that allows you to know when the recipient has received your message. Print out or save this message and put it in your file. You may need backup at a later time.

364. **Always virus check before you open a file onto your system—especially if you're on a network and could potentially infect your whole department or company.** The "Love Bug" virus in 2000 practically brought corporate America to its knees for two days. If you're the person who opens it and spreads it to your network, you are going to feel foolish and look unprofessional. A good rule of thumb is to never open an attachment from someone you don't know.

365. **Make sure you send uncorrupted files.** If you need to e-mail or share files, make sure you have a good anti-virus program. It's rude and inconsiderate to send unsafe files.

366. **Keep your e-mail messages short and simple.** The guideline for an e-mail message is about one screen, which is usually about twenty-five lines.

367. **Use short paragraphs.** It's hard to concentrate on a long paragraph printed on a piece of paper. It's even more difficult on a computer screen.

368. **Always use a subject line.** This will help your reader focus on your topic. Some people ignore messages without them.

369. **Don't use all capital letters.** The e-mail equivalent of shouting, capital letters, are also more difficult to read. The CEO of a company would use all caps to e-mail employees because he had bad eyesight. The employees

were still annoyed because his messages were hard to read. Why didn't he just wear his glasses? they wondered.

370. **Limit each message to one subject area.**

371. **Proofread every time.** Mistakes will be noticed and, depending upon the recipient, you may be judged for making them. Keep in mind that it's more difficult to proof on a screen. Read out loud slowly from the screen to catch your mistakes or print out the message and read it from a hard copy. Use your spell checker. If your e-mail program doesn't have a spell check feature, copy and paste the body of your message into your word processing program and spell check it there.

372. **Don't send or receive personal e-mails at work.** Before you start messaging your friends about your wild weekend or latest romantic liaison, remember, e-mail is not always private. Others may have access to your messages. Many companies are monitoring their e-mail systems and reprimanding employees for using e-mail for personal use. It's easy to set up a personal e-mail address at home.

373. **Don't send an e-mail message containing any business information that you want to keep confidential.** You don't know who may see the message once it's sent.

374. **Don't write anything about anyone that you wouldn't say directly to that person.** Though there may be times you want to say something in writing first, the general guideline is to not use e-mail as a way to avoid having a confrontation or a difficult conversation, such as reprimanding or firing someone (see page 131 for more information on how to handle sticky situations).

375. **Don't e-mail when you're angry or upset.** It's too easy to send the message and you may regret it later. At the very

least, give yourself a twenty-four-hour cooling off period and then decide if you still want to send the message.

376. **Don't e-mail thank-you notes.** E-mail does not replace
situations that have always required a handwritten
thank-you note. Stationery and your handwriting
make it more personal, though in some situations, a
quick note of thanks on e-mail can be effective.

SALUTATIONS AND CLOSINGS:

377. **Salutations and closings are not technically required
with e-mail.** Since e-mail is in memo format it does have
the sender's and receiver's names at the top of the screen.

378. **For internal messages, it's acceptable to use only first
names, as in simply "Jane."** Occasionally you will use
"Dear Jane" if you want to be more formal.

379. **For external messages, you can use just first names, as
in "Tom, " "Dear Tom" or "Dear Mr. Jones" as a salutation depending upon how formal your relationship is.**

380. **It's acceptable to use a closing if you use "Dear" in the
salutation.** Use "Sincerely" or "Best regards" depending upon your relationship. (See page 127 for more in-
depth information on closings.)

381. **Use your signature feature.** Some e-mail systems even
allow you to attach your signature.Many people choose to
also attach their name, phone number, and possibly even a
website link, automatically to the bottom of a message.

382. **Don't use e-mail symbols in your closing.** Not every
one understands the meaning of symbols like :) (it's a
smiley face) that many people use to close their e-mails.

Telephone Etiquette

"I can't stand when my boss answers the phone when I'm in his office in a meeting with him. He is telling me that I am not important!"

383. **Return phone calls within a day.** People who take a week or more or just don't bother to return a phone call is a complaint I hear a lot. People hate it when others don't return phone calls. And in some professions if you don't return the call immediately you could lose the sale.

384. **Don't answer your phone while you have a visitor in your office.** This doesn't involve new technology, but it occurs a lot and it's rude. You are telling your visitor that the person on the phone is more important than him or her. Unless you are expecting a very important call, let voice mail take a message. And if you do pick up, let the person know why you have to answer, such as, "I'm expecting a call from my boss." This is also true if you are meeting with colleagues or subordinates, if someone informally stops in your office, or when you are with others and your cell phone is turned on (see below for additional information on cell phone use.)

385. **Don't place people on hold without asking permission.** The person may not have time to wait. Also, don't ask if you can place someone on hold and then do it without waiting for an answer.

386. **Don't leave someone on hold without giving updates.** People do get nervous when put on hold for a long period of time. They think they've been forgotten. Give the person the option of continuing to hold or calling back at another time.

387. **Do not use call waiting in business!**

388. **Don't stalk your co-workers while they're on the phone.** It's rude. Even if you're out of earshot, it's still rude. You'll distract the person. Leave a note or stop back later. If the person had wanted to see you, signal the person that you are available.

389. **Don't interrupt others when they're on the phone.** This seems like a no-brainer but the participants of my seminars tell me people do this all time. One woman's boss just barges right in and starts talking to her as if the phone in her hand is invisible. She resents him! If it is very important, signal the person that you need to speak with him or her or leave a note.

390. **Let a caller know who else is in the room when the speakerphone is being used.** It can be embarrassing if the caller says something thinking only you were hearing it.

391. **Don't use a speakerphone if you share office space with others.** Your co-workers can hear your conversations and it's annoying and a distraction.

392. **Treat conference calls like regular meetings.** Be on time and be prepared. Participate but don't hog the conversation. It can be tempting to keep on talking since you can't see that others are eager to talk also.

393. **Whoever is hosting the conference call should make sure everyone on a conference call knows who all the other participants are.** Introductions should be made.

394. **Don't sneak out of a conference call.** You think you can run to the restroom or the copier and no one will know, but you might get found out. You will look like you don't care about the meeting and may offend the other participants.

395. **If you have Caller ID, don't answer using the person's name.** You may be wrong! Someone else may be using the person's phone. A woman answered, "What do you want!" to her boss. Her boss was using her friend's phone!

Smart Cellular Telephone Use

"The president of my daughter's university was welcoming the freshman class during their orientation. His phone rang. He answered and spoke. The students were insulted."

396. **Don't let your cell phone ring when sharing space with others.** Put it on vibrate. That means in a meeting, in a restaurant, on the train, etc. It's disturbing to others! Unbelievable but true: I was at a wedding and when the couple were saying their vows someone's cell phone went off!

397. **If you are in a crowded area and receive a call, leave the room to talk.** It's never good manners to broadcast your conversations.

398. **If you are by yourself and think that you are far enough away from others, you still must remember to speak in your quiet, normal voice.** Don't shout! It is amazing how many people broadcast their conversations.

399. **If you are doing the calling, let the person you're speaking with know you're calling from your cell phone.** Cellular telephone technology is good, but not perfect and you can suddenly be cut off.

400. **Never discuss sensitive or confidential information on your cellular telephone.** Eavesdropping technology is advanced too and you never know who might be standing by and listening.

401. **Use extreme caution when using your cell phone in your car.** Don't dial while you're driving. Unless you have a hands-free headset or speakerphone, wait until you've stopped. It's dangerous to hold a phone, talk and drive all at the same time. It's always a better idea to pull over to the side of the road or into a parking lot. When driving let voice mail answer your calls. Return them later.

402. **Use a regular telephone for important calls and clients.** A human resources director told me that a job candidate called on his cell phone to follow up after his interview. She could hear the traffic whooshing by and his phone cut out when he went under a bridge. In her mind, he was treating the call casually by not making the time or effort to call her from a regular phone.

403. **You also need to check your cell phone messages regularly,** even when you're in the office and using your regular phone.

Voice Mail Essentials

"I told a sales person that I was too busy to talk to him when he called but to please call back as I was interested in his service. He has since left me about ten voice mail messages. I feel like I'm being stalked. He's not going to get my business now."

WHEN YOU'RE THE CALLER:

404. **Don't speak too fast.** When leaving a message, slow down! The number one complaint people have about voice mail messages is that the caller speaks too quickly. The receiver has to replay the message several times in order to understand it.

405. **Always leave your name and number at least twice during the message, preferably at the beginning *and* at the end of the message.** You can't assume that the person you're calling remembers your phone number or is accessing their voice mail from his or her office. Plus you save the person from looking it up and people appreciate this small courtesy.

406. **Give enough information in your message.** If you can, give the reason for the call. This will help eliminate telephone tag. That way when the person returns the call, he or she can provide the information you needed whether you are there or not.

407. **Assume the person will answer.** Some people call when they think they'll get someone's voice mail, but you never know....Always be prepared to have a conversation or you will seem unprofessional. And don't say, "Oh, you're there, I thought I was going to get your voice mail." One of my clients told me when anyone says that she always thinks, "So why are you calling me if you don't think I'm here!"

408. **Don't fill up another person's voice mail with messages.** Nothing is going to turn a potential client off faster than being left several voice messages. Yet voice mail is not perfect—messages do get erased and systems malfunction. If after one message you don't hear

from the person, call again after a reasonable amount of time.

409. **Don't use a voice mail system to introduce yourself to someone you've never met.** You should do that in person or at least during a live telephone conversation.

410. **Don't use a voice mail system to get out of having difficult conversations.** Never offer condolences, convey confidential or critical information or criticize or fire someone using voice mail.

411. **Offer the caller the option to speak to a live person.** Many voice mail systems now give you the option to let the caller leave a message and then reach a live person. This is important if your clients and customers depend on you to solve last-minute problems.

Record A Winning Voice Mail Message:

412. **Say hello.** It's amazing the number of voice mail messages that fail to use this common courtesy. Identify yourself by your full name.

413. **Record your message when there are no distracting noises in the background.**

414. **Keep your message short.** But you don't want to say, "This is Barbara, leave a message." That's too abrupt. Be sure to offer information on how your system works and when you will be available to return calls.

415. **Be friendly and upbeat in your message.** I once called one of my clients and her voice mail message sounded so sad and morose. It made me wonder if something had happened.

416. **Be sure to keep your message up to date.** If you tell

your callers you are out of the office until a certain date, make sure that your callers don't hear the old message the day after your return to the office.

417. **Check your voice mail regularly.** This is especially important if you're out of the office a lot and if clients need to get a hold of you quickly.

418. **No cutesy stuff or musical numbers or singing in the background.** Save your creative messages for your home answering machine or voice mail system.

Videoconferencing

"I spent days preparing my presentation. As soon as the video-conference began I was told the people on the other end couldn't read any of my visual aids. It was very embarrassing. After the meeting was over my boss asked me how I could have overlooked a detail like that. I never will again!"

419. **Remember that unlike other people, the camera is always watching you.** So watch out for those nervous and fidgety gestures, such as doodling and paper clip twisting. Even meaningful, purposeful gestures can appear exaggerated on the screen.

420. **Dress as if your whole body will be showing.** A man wore sneakers to a videoconference, thinking the camera would only see his upper half...it caught his whole body. He was very embarrassed.

421. **Speak to the camera.** During a videoconference I participated in, one of the participants looked down at his

notes the whole time. It made it harder to understand him and he seemed rude.

422. **Be animated.** Smile.

423. **Be totally prepared.** Dead sound is bad enough with a live group but over a videoconference, it's particularly bad.

424. **Make sure any visual aids will be able to be seen over the screen.**

MISCELLANEOUS TECHNO-ETIQUETTE

Pagers should be on vibrate when you're around other people, most especially if you're in a meeting.

Palm Pilot and electronic organizers have alarms that can be annoying to others. Make sure you turn this feature off when you're in a meeting.

Don't program your Palm Pilot or electronic organizer as you're walking around. A woman told me that her co-worker was programming his as he was coming off the elevator and banged right into her. It was rude and it hurt!

Don't surf the Net for personal reasons while at work. More and more companies are cracking down on this behavior. Remember too, you leave a trail of every site you visit. I recently heard of a manager who was fired from a car manufacturer for viewing pornographic sites on his work computer.

Don't import and play computer games to your computer at work. You will look very unprofessional if you get caught playing network hearts or chess.

Don't change the settings on other people's computers without their permission. If you have to use or borrow a co-worker's computer station, leave every computer setting exactly as you found it. Don't forget to put the keyboard tray and chair height back into position too. One secretary told me that she wasted over two hours because her computer wasn't printing and she was trying to troubleshoot the printer. It turns out that someone used her computer and changed the printer setting to print on the other side of the office.

≈SEVEN≈

BUSINESS WRITING BASICS

*Before You Write * Once You Begin Writing * Guidelines for Selecting Successful Salutations * Guidelines For Selecting Successful Salutations * Choose the Right Closing * Making Sure Your Business Writing Has the Right Look * Guideline for Thank You Notes * Business Writing FAQs*

"After a tough round of interviewing, we felt confident that we had found our new director—until the candidate sent us a follow-up letter thanking us for the interview. There were three typos in the letter, and a few very awkwardly worded sentences. We chose someone else for the job."

WE LIVE AND WORK in an age of advanced technology—faxes, modems, and e-mail—that has dramatically changed how we communicate. But one thing that hasn't changed is the importance of our words and the absolute necessity to write them effectively. Words have power, and written words have lasting power.

No matter whether it's a letter sent by regular mail or via the new technological vehicles, putting your thoughts in writing makes a statement not only about your writing ability and the state of your communications skills, but about who you are as a professional. When you communicate in writing to co-workers, bosses, vendors, customers, or clients, you reveal a great deal about yourself and, because you're a representative of your organization, the company you work for. You reveal if you're someone with a good grasp of language. You reveal if you're someone who cares about quality. You reveal if you're a person who attends to the details—or not.

A poorly written letter to a potential client can have disastrous effects on your business relationships and, ultimately, your career. A bank sent out letters to its customers to assure them that they were in compliance for Y2K. There were typos in the letter. Their customers were not assured! The bank's president received many complaints. He was mortified and angry. The Y2K compliance manager was severely criticized.

You may be willing to overlook certain mistakes and not hold it against the writer, but trust me, many others do. I have had participants in my seminars say they are not good with spelling or grammar and so they can overlook those errors in other people's writing. Yet, as they are saying those words, others in the class are rolling their eyes and saying that the same errors mattered a great deal to them!

It's critical that your written words consistently say that you are an effective communicator.

You don't have to be a professional writer to write a successful business letter, memo or report. Though writing is not a skill that comes naturally to everyone, like any skill it can be learned. Your writing can, and will, significantly improve with a solid understanding of the process and, of course, with lots of practice.

BEFORE YOU WRITE:

425. Know why you are writing. You usually write to clarify the finer points of a contract, to persuade a potential client to do business with you, to give out information or to complain. Be clear about your purpose. It will help you get your words down on paper.

426. **Know your audience.** Be clear about who you are addressing and what their level or depth of knowledge is. Visualizing your reader can also help you get your words down on paper.

427. **Ask yourself, do I have to write?** Is a face-to-face meeting or a phone call possible and would it accomplish more? A consultant was sending status reports to her client, yet every time she spoke to him he wanted her to give him a verbal update. He valued hearing from her more than the written report.

428. **Don't reinvent the wheel with every letter.** Most of the business letters and memos you write will share common characteristics. Each has a purpose. Each has a beginning, middle, and an end. Each should have a professional "look." In other words, most business letters share a common organization that you can use as a model. Find other letters or memos that you know were successful and use them as guides. Analyze the structure and wording and you will greatly enhance the effectiveness of your writing.

429. **Schedule a specific time to write.** This is especially important if you find that business writing is more difficult than other aspects of your job. Schedule a time when you know you'll be relatively undisturbed and feel clear-headed. This will help you get your words down on paper more easily. I like to write in the morning. I feel clear-headed and full of energy. I know it's a good time to tackle tough projects.

430. **Give yourself a deadline.** A realistic deadline can help you be more productive in both starting your writing project and completing it. A writer I know tells me that unless her editor gives her a deadline, she never completes the project!

431. **Think about your reader.** The more you know about the person you're writing to, the easier it will be to write to him or her effectively. Are you writing to someone who relishes even the smallest details of a project? Someone who likes to get down to business quickly? If you have written correspondence from the person you're writing to, study it and keep it handy as you write. Such writing samples can provide you with clues on how best to communicate with your reader.

432. **Try the clustering technique.** If you find writer's block to be a problem, clustering can help you get started. It's designed to help you find out what you know about a topic, and what areas may need additional research or information. Put your main topic in the center of a piece of paper. Then, let your thoughts and ideas flow unedited. Write down any and all phrases and points that come to mind in clusters around the key words. Later, you can delete what you don't need and then organize your clusters when it's time to write a first draft.

433. **Don't expect to get it right on the first draft.** Putting your words down on paper so others understand them can take time.

ONCE YOU BEGIN WRITING:

434. **Use the open writing technique to help get started.** The idea is to open yourself up and simply let the words

flow. Don't cross out or revise anything until you get through your whole letter or report once. Allow yourself to make mistakes. Many people find they get blocked from getting the words down on paper because they're so worried about what they're writing and how good—or bad—it sounds. Remember, no one else will see this first draft. It's your private tool for helping you write better.

435. **Write the way you speak.** You are writing to people, not file cabinets. So write in a conversational tone. When you speak you wouldn't say, "Pursuant to our conversation, enclosed please find the information on our new product that you requested." You would say, "Here is the information you requested on our new product."

436. **Rewrite.** Remember, it may take you several drafts to get your words to flow.

437. **Understand that the quality of your writing always counts.** Don't make the mistake of thinking, "Oh this is just a quick note or fax, it's not like a formal letter." Many of my students send me copies of the ridiculous letters they receive. They also send them on to others or post them on the bulletin boards for all to see! If it's for business, the quality of your writing always matters and you will be judged for it. (For specific e-mail guidelines see pages 102.)

438. **Vary the length of your paragraphs.** If all the paragraphs are the same length, your document will be boring to read. If all of your paragraphs are long, the document becomes a sheet of black ice and the readers' eyes slide right over it. Keep paragraphs as short as you can; brevity enhances readability. As a general guideline paragraphs should be nine lines or less.

439. **Vary the length of your sentences.** And keep them short. Average sentence length is fifteen to seventeen words but you can use longer or shorter sentences. A one- or two-word sentence can be effective. Why not! But very long sentences can confuse the reader. One manager had an employee count the words in his sentences to stop him from using fifty-word sentences.

440. **Use bullets if and when possible.** Bullets are an effective way to highlight important information and break up blocks of text.

441. **Eliminate extra words.** One of the biggest complaints people have about business letters is that most use too many words. Time is precious. Don't squander your time or your reader's by filling your letter with unnecessary words. Why say, "Thanking you in advance for your kind attention to this matter" when "Thank you" does the trick?

442. **Use "you" when you're writing, as it provides a reader focus.** Your words need to help you establish a relationship with the reader. "You asked about the new software" is more personal than "Enclosed please find information on the new software."

443. **Use everyday words.** Big words don't always impress people. They might even intimidate or annoy your reader. Even if the reader knows what a word means, he or she might have to think about it for a minute, which detracts from your message. Instead, use simple words that say exactly what you mean. Why use "annihilate" when "eliminate" will do?

444. **You can use contractions.** When we speak we use contractions, so it is permissible to do so in business writ-

ing. Contractions also help you keep a more conversational tone in your writing. But *don't* overdo it!

445. **Be careful with humor.** Humor can be a great personal touch to add to a business letter. But humor in writing can also be harder to pull off than in person because you don't have the benefit of non-verbal signals to help get your meaning across. If there's any chance you may offend someone, keep the joke to yourself.

446. **Avoid sexist phrasing.** Many people, for the sake of convenience, will favor masculine pronouns and possessives. "A person needs to feel like he has job security" should be changed to "People need to feel like they have job security."

447. **Avoid negative phrasing.** "If we ever get the project off the ground" is a negative statement. "When we get this project off the ground" is a more positive choice of phrasing. "You neglected to sign the contract" could put your reader on the defensive; "Please remember to sign contracts in the future" is a more positive way of getting your point across.

448. **Write a good opening sentence.** Your opening sentence needs to grab the reader's attention and get to the point. The opening often determines whether your letter gets read or not. But don't get hung up on the opening. If you're stuck, move on. You can always go back and write it after you have done your first draft.

449. **Be creative.** Depending on the purpose of your letter or your relationship with the recipient you may want to get more creative in your opening. A direct mail letter, for example, uses openings that appeal to emotions: "Your company is spending $100,000 a year more

than you have to on promotions. How would you like to be the hero who comes up with the cost-cutting solution?"

450. **Don't make mistakes!** A typo, a misused word, or a confusing sentence in your letter can undermine your credibility. A computer company's proposal for a million-dollar project was turned down because there were typos in the document.

TO ENSURE THAT YOUR BUSINESS WRITING IS FREE OF MISTAKES:

451. **Read your document out loud.** Many editors and professional writers rely on this rule. Where you stumble over your own words, the reader will stumble. If it doesn't sound right to you, chances are it won't sound right to your reader. Learn to trust your ear. If something in your letter doesn't sound right or flow smoothly, change it. And you must read out loud. Reading silently isn't as effective as actually hearing how your words sound.

452. **Let someone else read your letter.** It's often hard to catch your own mistakes. Be open to feedback and suggestions.

453. **Use an up-to-date style manual.** When I ask participants in my writing seminars where they get the rules, I'm often told they rely on memories of high school grammar classes. Bad idea! The rules may have changed or you may not be remembering it correctly. A style manual explains the rules of grammar, punctuation, and some even offer writing guidelines. If you don't know something, look it up! Good choices include Strunk and White's *Elements of Style* or the *Gregg Reference Manual.*

454. Identify your weak spots. We all make mistakes and most of us make the same ones over and over again, like typing "your" instead of "you're," because we're unaware of our own patterns. Start tracking your mistakes. Keep a list and when you repeat one, put a check mark by it. Over time, you'll be able to spot your patterns and catch the mistakes you make most often.

455. Use your computer's spell check and grammar guide— always. Most word-processing programs allow you to customize the features.

GUIDELINES FOR SELECTING SUCCESSFUL SALUTATIONS:

456. Choose the right salutation for your letter or memo. The salutation is one of the most important elements of the business letter. If you offend the recipient in the first line, he or she may not continue to read your letter. I know a man whose name is Charles. He told me if he gets a letter addressed to "Dear Chuck" he throws it away.

457. Use the correct name and title. An incorrect name or title offends many people. Call the company to get the person's name and title and ask the receptionist to spell the name for you.

458. Use last names if you don't know the person or have spoken to them only once or twice. Even though we can be an informal society, it is usually better to err on the side of formality.

459. Use first names if you're sure it's okay to do so. If you know the person, have been asked to call the person by his or her first name or you receive a letter that the writer signed with his or her first name only—then it's fine to use a first name.

460. **Don't use nicknames unless you know it is okay.** A woman I know is very offended if she gets a letter addressed to Dear Margie. She wants to be called Marjorie.

461. **Avoid "Dear Sir/Ms."** You are telling the reader that you haven't a clue as to who he or she is. Though Ms. is the preferred term in business today, not every woman likes to be called "Ms." If you are unsure of whether to use Ms. or Mrs. and think you might offend the person if you guess wrong, just use the first and last name—"Dear Sally Jones."

462. **When it's impossible to know or include the recipient's name, use a non-gender-specific, non-sexist term such as "client," "customer," "participant," "representative," etc.** You can add "representative" to virtually every department name, as in "Dear Sales Representative." In most situations, it works quite well.

463. **Avoid Gentleman.** A nun once told me that she has gotten more than one letter addressed to "Dear Gentleman." What was that writer thinking?

464. **When in doubt about the person's gender, use both the recipient's first and last name.** With a name such as Pat Smith, use both the first and last name and drop the Ms. or Mr., such as "Dear Pat Smith."

465. **Avoid "To Whom it May Concern."** Most letters addressed this way are thrown away. Even if the letter is saved, it could take weeks to actually find the person it may concern.

CHOOSE THE RIGHT CLOSING:

466. **The closing needs to be in sync with the salutation.** You wouldn't start a letter with an informal salutation

like "Dear Sally" and end with the formal closing, "Respectfully yours." Use the following closings as guidelines:

467. **"Respectfully" and "Respectfully yours."** These terms are used when corresponding with government officials or members of the clergy.

468. **"Very truly yours."** A more formal closing used with last names.

469. **"Sincerely" and "Sincerely yours."** These are the most frequently used closings for business contacts and can be used with first or last names.

470. **"Best regards," and "Regards."** These are informal, but acceptable in some business situations where there's a high degree of familiarity and first names are used.

471. **Be cautious with the use of P.S.** The postscript was originally used as a way to include material left out of the letter without retyping the entire document. Some people now consider it an afterthought and don't understand why a writer would use it with today's word processing technology and the ability to make changes with ease. You will most often find a P.S. in a sales or direct mail letter, where it is used to reemphasize an important point. But for most business correspondence, a P.S. is no longer necessary.

MAKING SURE YOUR BUSINESS WRITING HAS THE RIGHT LOOK:

472. **Know your company's guidelines.** Many companies today provide templates for their employees to use for memos and faxes. Formal business letters usually go on good quality letterhead.

473. **Make sure you use a good quality second sheet if your letter or memo is more than one page long.** A banking executive told me he received an important letter that had the second page printed on plain white paper, which contrasted greatly with the first page. He noticed and was very turned off by it. "He was obviously not paying attention to the details," he said of the sender.

474. **Check your margins.** Again, you must always consider your letter's readability. 1" to 1" margins on all sides are recommended for most letters.

475. **Don't forget to sign your letter.** It's extremely unprofessional to forget your signature. People appreciate an actual, legible signature. Some will even check to make sure your signature is not a stamp.

476. **Don't overuse the emphasis techniques.** Computers allow you to do all sorts of visual effects. Don't let your letters become ransom notes:

> —This is the RANSOM note *style* of a <u>letter.</u> I have put **everything** in here that my computer CAN DO!

477. **Look for imperfections.** One smudge or an unnecessary crease on your letter may lead the recipient to think you are careless and don't pay attention to the details.

GUIDELINES FOR THANK-YOU NOTES:

478. **Send a thank-you note when appropriate—when you receive a gift, go to a party or a meal.** You can also

send thank-you notes to people who provide extra help for you or when you want to praise an employee or vendor.

479. **Timing is everything.** The note should be sent within twenty-four hours of the party or receipt of the gift. Allowing much more time to pass will cause your thank you to lose some meaning.

480. **If you have legible handwriting, a thank-you note should be handwritten.** It's more personal. If you are writing to someone to thank him or her after a job interview or sales call, you are usually writing a thank-you letter. Generally for this type of thank you, you would type the letter since it is usually a much longer, more detailed writing.

481. **Keep it short.** Three to five sentences is an appropriate length.

482. **Use a good quality notepaper.** Ideally, you want to use 5-by-7 inch notepaper, or folded paper. It should have your company name on it but it shouldn't look too official. You don't want it to be too cute either.

BUSINESS WRITING FAQS

Q: Does the period always go inside the closing quote?

A: Many participants in my writing seminars complain that this rule makes no sense. I tell them, you're right! It doesn't make sense but that's the rule—always. There are no exceptions to this rule. And, "I mean it."

Q: Should I capitalize management titles, such as, "The President announced a new price increase?"

A: Generally, the answer is no. You don't usually capitalize management titles, such as "The president announced a new price increase," but some companies do for emphasis or to show respect. Best advice: Follow your company's guidelines.

Q: What's the difference between "who" and "that"?
A: Use either "who" or "that" in conjunction with a person and use "that" when referring to things.

Q: If "etc." is the last word of a sentence, do I use two periods?
A: No. The period from "etc." serves as the ending period. I discourage people from using this expression in business writing. It's usually more effective to be more specific.

Q: Some people say it's one comma in a series of three items, but others say two. What's correct?
A: Both. It depends upon which style manual you follow—and you should follow one. Some say one comma is correct, others say two. In fact, people will defend to the death their position that one is more correct than the other. The important thing is to adhere to your company's style and to remain consistent.

❧ EIGHT ❧

HANDLING STICKY SITUATIONS

*What Type of Confronter Are You? * Learn How Not to Create Conflict ** Giving Feedback and Criticism to Others * Giving Embarrassing News To Others * Giving Difficult News to Others * Quitting Your Job*

"I really wanted to say something. I just didn't know how."

WHAT DO YOU DO about the annoying, distracting, or bothersome behaviors of others?

Do you complain about him or her to your other colleagues? But never say a word to the offending person! Many people do this.

Do you seethe with silent anger? Do you swear to yourself, "Next time, I'll say something!"? But then the next time comes and you can't seem to find the words then either. Do you bang your fist on the desk and explode at the person? Many people do these things too.

But there is a better alternative. There is a better way to deal with the bothersome behavior of others.

Most people are never taught how to confront others effectively using what I call polite and powerful behavior. But you can learn the skills—once you know what they are. If you practice (remember, you can't transform yourself overnight!) the skills outlined in this section you will feel better about yourself because you won't feel like a huge wimp or the person who lost her "cool" again. Practice the skills I talk about here and you will feel more confident in your ability to confront people.

Confronting others in a way that can get their bothersome behavior to stop, reduce your at-work stress, enhance your people skills, make you look more professional, and feel good is what this section is all about. I should note: much of the information in this chapter can be found in much greater detail in my book, *The Power of Positive Confrontation*—I encourage you to read it for more in-depth knowledge about handling conflict effectively.

WHAT TYPE OF CONFRONTER ARE YOU?

#1. The Complainer. "Complainer" is a nice way of saying "wimp." (This used to be me.) This person doesn't confront the person who is saying or doing something bothersome. But he or she needs to complain in order to get relief from bad feelings. And does this person complain—to friends, family, co-workers—anyone who will listen will suffice. Unfortunately, the relief a Complainer feels is often short-lived.

#2. The Avoider. These are wimps who will do just about anything not to have a confrontation with people who may be bothering them. They say, "It's not that big of an issue," when it *is* an issue. Their motto is "Why rock the boat?" Often they don't just avoid having a confrontation, they avoid the other person, too. It's easier, they think, than hurting someone's feelings.

#3. The Pretender. Denial, denial, denial. Pretenders accept things that they wouldn't if they were honest. Unlike the Avoider, the

Pretender can't even admit he or she has difficult feelings. Sadly, these are also people whose health suffers, often chronically.

#4. The Bully. Unfortunately, the kid who crushed your lunch box has grown up, is still a bully, and is now in the working world or living next door! This is the person who says, "She had it coming!" to justify his or her behavior. The Bully must get his or her way and will often become aggressive if, and when, challenged. He or she is frustrated and doesn't know how to express it other than through aggressive behavior. This person wants to win. End of discussion.

#5. The Shouter. A Shouter is not happy about what is going on, and the only way he or she knows how to express his or her displeasure is by shouting, then shouting some more. Sometimes people become Shouters by accident. These are people who approach a conflict with the best of intentions, but their behavior doesn't match their intentions. They get upset and they lose control. And then they shout.

#6. The Self-Discounter. This person, by his or her verbal or nonverbal communication, negates a positive intention: "Gee, sorry. Well, you know how sensitive I am…" or "This is probably just my problem, but…" or "I think kinda, maybe, sort of, what's bothering me could be…." Or this person is saying, "I'm offended by the comment," and the offending person can't hear her because she has her head down and her voice lowered.

#7. The Displacer. This is the person who suffers in silence—for a while—then BAM. The Displacer ignores the real issue and reaches the boiling point and then blows a lid about another issue. True feelings leak out one way or another, sometimes to areas of conflict that seem safer.

So Who Are You? The point of these seven profiles is not so you cast yourself as this or that type. It's to help you become more aware of some all-too-common negative behaviors. You may also have recognized yourself in more than one profile. That's very common. Just remember, with some practice you can develop a new and better way to approach confrontation.

WHEN ANOTHER PERSON'S BEHAVIOR IS ANNOYING OR BOTHERSOME:

483. **Understand that you have the right to speak up and say something if another person's behavior is bothersome or annoying.** If you're nervous about speaking up, pretend that you're not. Eventually, the inside will catch up to your confident outward appearance. I call this "faking it until you feel it."

484. **Understand what kind of confronter you are.** Whether or not you know it, you do have a confrontational style. Tuning into your style is your first step in changing it. (See box on page 134.)

485. **Take the jerk test.** If your co-worker is doing something that's bugging you, like playing the radio too loudly, ask yourself, "Does this person really mean any harm?" It could be that he or she has no clue that his or her behavior is even bothersome to others. What may seem obvious to you may not be obvious to someone else. Though there are true "jerks" out there, I've found that most people aren't out to get you. You just need to tell the person what the difficulty is—in a polite and powerful way.

486. **Before confronting the other person, plan what you are going to say.** Many people get tongue-tied when it comes to having a confrontation. But if you plan your words, you'll be more confident.

DON'T ATTACK 'EM, WAC'EM™ INSTEAD

This very simple yet effective model helps you get your words together so when you do choose to say something, you are more apt to be polite and powerful. While you're getting more comfortable with having positive confrontations, I suggest writing down your wording so you can practice.

W = What.   What's *really* bothering you? Define the problem.

A = Ask.   What do you want to ask the other person to do or change? Define what would solve the problem for you.

C = Check in. You need to check in with the other person and get the other person's reaction.

Here's a simple scenario, yet it causes many difficulties in organizations. Here's the WAC'em approach applied to it:

Scenario: Your co-worker spends a lot of time organizing his social life on the phone. It's very distracting to listen to.

WAC'em Wording: The W stands for WHAT. *What's really bothering you?* Define the problem. How will you express it to the other person? You must explain specifically what that person is doing.

"We sit close together so there isn't much privacy. I can hear most of your conversations and they're distracting."

The A stands for ASK. *What do you want to ask the other person to do or change?* Have a specific solution or action in mind before saying anything.

"I would appreciate it if you could lower your voice when you are on the phone."

The C stands for CHECK IN. *Check in with the other person to get his or her reaction.* You need to find out if the other person can and will do what you ask. Be open-minded the other person may have some good ideas too.

Okay.

487. **Don't label the other person's behavior:** "You're so *inconsiderate* to leave on time when the rest of the team is pulling extra hours." "You're *selfish* for never chipping in on office gifts." These kinds of labels will go nowhere quickly. Labeling only serves to make the other person feel defensive.

488. **Use "I" not "You" statements.** "You" statements can blame or attack the other person. "You never have the report done on time" or "I need the weekly report by 10:30 Monday morning." Or "You are not listening" or " I need you to concentrate on this."

489. **Don't make apologies or excuses.** "I'm so sorry to bug you about this. I know I'm such a big fat pain. But I'm very, very sensitive to sound. I can't focus on my work when you play your radio." You don't need to put yourself down in order to speak up.

490. **Use softening statements, when appropriate.** You can give the person the benefit of the doubt by using a statement such as, "I'm sure you mean no harm..." or "I know you mean well..."

491. **Be aware of your body language.** Don't wind your body up into a knot or use nervous gestures. Watch your volume. If you speak too softly, you will seem wimpy. If you shout, you'll seem like a bully.

492. **Pick the right time to approach the person and speak privately.** Don't try to talk to him or her when he or she may be running late or on a tight deadline. Don't confront at happy hour either. You may think that having a drink helps you relax, but it can also help the conversation get sidetracked or out of hand.

493. **Try to reach an agreement.** If the person doesn't want to give you exactly what you want, can you meet somewhere in the middle?

494. **Listen to the other person.** Be open and receptive to hearing his or her point of view. Try using a clarifying statement, such as, "What is it about my request that you feel you can't do?" "What exactly do you find silly?" "Why are you saying that?"

495. **Follow up with yourself.** Evaluate how the confrontation went. What did you learn? How could it be improved? Each time you will get better at getting your words right and you won't feel so nervous.

496. **Follow up with the other person.** People don't change overnight. You may have to reinforce your point with the other person later. Review any agreements you made. Make adjustments if necessary. If the person changes their behavior, thank them for it.

497. **Feel good about yourself.** A few people may continue to be jerks and there may or may not be anything you can do about it. But at least if you do confront the person politely and powerfully, you can feel good about yourself that you spoke up.

498. **Consider your other options.** If you're bothered by a noisy co-worker, can your work area be moved? Are there rules in your company handbook? Can you go over the person's head and ask a boss or supervisor to intervene? Be careful about doing this, however, it could backfire on you. You may end up looking bad or like you can't solve your own problems.

Learn How Not to Create Conflict

"Our employees love our director. He always says hello to people as he walks down the hall. And boy they can't do enough for him."

499. **Learn how *not* to be a source of conflict for others.** Many of the essential things in this book will help you get along with others because as you now know, the little things can really add up. Be sure to review the tips and advice for building relationships on page 9.

500. **Greet and acknowledge others.** It's been said before, but the number one thing in my mind that will eliminate conflict is when you do this one thing! It is very simple; Say hello, good morning, have a nice day, etc.

501. **Be considerate when sharing work space.** If you mess up the conference room, clean it up. Don't leave your lunch in the refrigerator for three weeks. If you're the person at the copier when the paper runs out, refill it. It's these kind of annoying things that people do that drive others crazy.

502. **If someone confronts you, be willing to listen.** You may not realize that you've been a source of conflict or annoyance for another person.

Giving Feedback and Criticism to Others

"It was the first time a manager told me exactly what I needed to do to get promoted around here. Boy, it felt good to actually know what I was doing right and wrong."

503. **Make sure you are the appropriate person to give the feedback.** If you're the person's manager or team leader it is your job to give feedback. If it's not your job, be cautious with giving unsolicited advice. Many people are not open to it.

504. **Know your company's guidelines for giving employees critical feedback.** If someone is not performing to a standard, you may be required to document the conversation. You may be required to get input on the person's performance from others in the department. Your organization may provide forms and guidelines for evaluations. If there are procedures to follow, make sure you follow them.

505. **Always give critical feedback in private.** It's never appropriate to criticize someone's job performance in front of others.

506. **Be specific about what's wrong with the person's performance.** Don't expect anyone to hear "lousy" or "sloppy" and to understand exactly what you mean. Not only will the person get defensive upon hearing these negative labels, they may not have enough information to change the behavior. "Your last report had several typos" or "The catalog is late for the second time" are examples of specific behavior.

507. **Balance the negative with the positive.** If possible, try to say something good about the person's performance. It may help the person not become defensive. "These typos take away from your valuable conclusions."

508. **Tell someone how you expect him or her to change.** Again, be specific about the behavior or improvement you expect: "Your attendance at the weekly meeting is

mandatory" or "I'd like to see you contribute more at the weekly meeting."

509. **Give the person a deadline for improvement.** This may be dictated by company policy or it may be up to your discretion. Either way, make sure the person understands when the improvement is expected. Set a date for reevaluation.

510. **State the consequences.** It may be necessary to explain what's at stake if the person can't improve. Again, be specific: "You won't get the raise" or "You won't be ready for promotion."

511. **Hear what the person has to say.** You may be unaware of a situation that is preventing the person from getting the report on time. There may be extenuating circumstances that you don't know.

Giving Embarrassing News to Others

"I'm a guy—I just didn't know how to tell my boss, Nancy, that she had toilet paper stuck in her skirt so I didn't say anything. I let her walk around that way. When she finally discovered it, she was upset with me for not letting her know."

512. **Don't use innuendo or hand signals to deliver your message.** Simply describe the situation and do it quietly: "Tom, your fly is down" or "Mary, your slip is showing."

513. **Write the person a note.** If you feel like someone would be less embarrassed if you slipped him or her a note, then do so.

514. **If you're embarrassed because of gender send a same-sex emissary.**

515. **Say what you need to say then drop it.** Don't make jokes or bring it up later. You will look immature and unprofessional if you do.

516. **If you're the person whose fly is down or blouse open and someone tells you, simply zip up or button up and move on.** Accept that this kind of thing happens to everyone once in a while. Handle it with grace and good humor.

GIVING DIFFICULT NEWS TO OTHERS:

517. **Talk in private.** You don't announce in a crowded meeting that one of your team members didn't make employee of the year. You need to tell him or her privately first.

518. **Avoid making ominous statements.** Many people will say, "I don't know how to tell you this...." It's better to be direct and say, "I have some bad news..." or "There's been a change of plans..." and then just tell them quickly.

519. **Keep it simple.** Offer the reasons if you can. "Sally was chosen for the job as she had more experience in marketing."

520. **Stick to your position.** Be polite but powerful, even if the other person isn't. "We've made our decision. The next opening will be in about nine months. You can try again then."

521. **Give the person alternatives, or offer to help, if possible.** A boss told his employee that she didn't get the

promotion but helped her find a training class to improve the skills that were holding her back.

Quitting Your Job

"I am so glad that I practiced what I was going to tell my boss when I let him know I was leaving. If I hadn't, I might have lost my cool and said things I regretted."

522. **Practice what you're going to say.** If you write the words down ahead of time, chances are you will be less nervous. Get a friend to role-play with you.

523. **Don't apologize.** You can say, "I'm sad to be leaving this great group of people." This is not the same as saying, "I'm sorry, you're going to hate me for this, but...." Unless you've signed a contract, you have a right to leave your job.

524. **Don't use nervous non-verbal signals.** If you twist in your chair or play with your hair, you're not going to look like a person who has just made an important decision. You're going to look unsure and nervous.

525. **Don't give too much information.** Keep it simple. "I've decided to pursue another opportunity" is a fine explanation. You don't have to fill your boss in on all the details. How much you choose to share will depend upon your relationship with that person.

526. **Give sufficient notice.** You want to leave on good terms and one of the best ways to do this is to give your boss at least the minimum two weeks notice. Even if you

don't have a great relationship with your boss, the professional thing to do is to give two weeks notice. Some companies may prefer that you leave sooner and if that's the case, fine. Some people make an effort to give more time, especially if the relationship they've had with their boss is a good one.

527. **Be prepared for an argument.** If you think your boss may try to argue with you or try to talk you out of leaving, go in with a line you've already prepared. "I do appreciate your concern, and I've made my decision." No matter what the person says to you, just stick firmly to your line—unless it's an offer you can't refuse!

528. **Leave your bridges standing.** I know it's tempting, but don't do it! No matter how long you've fantasized about telling your boss off or setting the record straight—don't do it. You may feel wonderful for ten minutes afterwards, but later on, you'll probably feel bad about it. And the only thing you've accomplished is that you've lost a reference.

❧ NINE ❧

GLOBAL BUSINESS ISSUES

*When You're the Visitor * Plan For Differences In International
Presentations * Dress for International Success * When You're the Host *
Making Conversation the International Way * Dining Differences *
International Writing Differences * International Gift-Giving Guidelines*

THANKS TO THE Internet and to ever expanding trade relations
the world just keeps getting smaller—but not necessarily easier to understand. More American organizations are doing business
globally now than ever before. And yet, our knowledge of how to
do business internationally still lags behind, thanks at least in part
to the United States' physical isolation from other countries. Until
recently, when the US started becoming much more a multicultur-
al society, most of us lived with little or no exposure to other countries, cultures and customs. But ignorance is no excuse—American
business people working in a global arena need to be better trained
in international business etiquette and cultural awareness issues—
period.

Katherine, an American sales representative, giggled when her
Indian customer greeted her using the *namaste* (a traditional greeting with two hands together). She had no idea what he was doing

and she reacted inappropriately because she was nervous. "I knew immediately that I embarrassed him. I regretted it, but the damage was done," said Katherine. "We were uncomfortable with each other after that. I felt like all the work I spent establishing a rapport with him was lost the moment that giggle came out of my mouth."

Though eventually the sales representative was able to repair the relationship, the consequences of making international business etiquette mistakes can often be far more damaging, even if they're made in innocence. Bottom line: When you're doing business with clients, customers, vendors, managers, or co-workers from another country, ignorance of their protocols and business etiquette issues is simply not acceptable.

To operate successfully in the global business arena, you first need to be aware of cultural differences, and then to understand the impact those differences have on a country's way of doing business. When you know how to handle yourself in international business situations, you'll be more confident conducting your business and you'll project a positive impression about yourself and the organization you represent.

So what exactly are the rules? How do you know how to behave when traveling abroad or dealing with international business colleagues or clients at home? The answer is that etiquette varies from culture to culture. Yet there are basic guidelines that can help you successfully navigate the business globe. While this is by no means a definitive list, the information below does contain international etiquette essentials for all cultures and highlights issues that generally invite error.

When You're the Visitor

"My company sent me over to Saudi Arabia for six weeks. Thank goodness I had some cultural training before I went. The differ-

GLOBAL BUSINESS ISSUES

ence in lifestyles that I observed was amazing. I know I made some mistakes but not as many as I could have. My Saudi colleagues were impressed with what I did know and that helped me forge a stronger relationship with them."

529. Understand that you are the one who needs to adapt. You are the visitor; you must change or modify your behavior. We expect visitors to our country to adapt to our customs; we are expected to adapt to theirs. The old adage, "When in Rome, do as the Romans do" is absolutely true.

530. Get a good guidebook. Read and study before your trip. The more you know about a culture the easier it will be to adapt. There are many culture-specific guidebooks that provide in-depth information about other countries and their customs. Make sure the guidebook you select offers some key phrases and information about currency as well as customs. Read through it before you leave and bring it with you so you can use it there.

531. Surf the Net. You will find tons of information on other countries, customs, and cultures on the Internet. Use search engines and other electronic resources to find good, reliable information—ask a librarian or Web-savvy friend to help if you don't know where to begin.

532. Take advantage of any training opportunities your organization may provide. More and more organizations with global business interests are providing in-house training and seminars on different aspects of international business. Many universities also provide continuing education classes on international etiquette. I have taught an international business class at Penn State University. Many companies do pay tuition for this type of class.

533. **Make sure you have a good grasp of the basics.** Learn some of the geography and history of the country; religious beliefs and customs; local currency; key personalities, such as politicians and local celebrities; gift-giving etiquette; social structure, like the role of women; and business culture, such as the relationship between boss and subordinate.

534. **Make sure you're aware of any customs prohibitions for the country you're visiting.** Don't try to bring liquor into a country where it is against the religion.

535. **Learn global greetings.** And don't judge someone on the quality of his or her handshake. Not every culture shakes hands and if they do it is not always the way we do. In other parts of the word you may kiss, hug or bow.

536. **Don't expect other business cultures to do business the "American way."** Many cultures do not place the same emphasis on the value of work or have the same management styles. You may go overseas and want to "get right down to business." But remember, this is an American business value, not necessarily shared by other business cultures.

537. **Understand that in many business cultures, you must establish a personal relationship before you can do business.** Don't be impatient with this "getting to know you" step; it builds trust. You may even spend a lot of time socializing—maybe more than you want—but again, it can be a necessary part of establishing the needed relationship.

538. **Don't react negatively to another person's customs.** Chances are, if you're doing business globally, you will

encounter customs that you'll find very different, even shocking. It's important to respect the differences. Remember you are the visitor. Sometimes you can say, "That's very different from what we experience in the United States."

539. **Don't brag about American culture.** This is considered rude.

540. **Accept invitations.** A sales representative was invited to his Indian customer's daughter's birthday party. He didn't want to spend his afternoon at a kid's party so he didn't go. The customer was so insulted he threatened to pull his account.

541. **Expect differences in non-verbal communication.** Try to mentally prepare for these differences so they won't interfere with your ability to listen and understand.

542. **Know how much eye contact is appropriate.** In the U.S., you are encouraged to look someone directly in the eye while speaking to that person. But in some cultures, Asian for example, looking away is a sign of respect. Still other cultures, like the French for example, may look more intently at you than you are used to.

543. **Know how much space to give others.** When conversing with someone, you need to be aware that your proximity to the person is also dictated by custom. In some cultures, like Argentina and Italy, you will be closer than the average U.S. distance of approximately three feet. And in other cultures, like Japan, you will be farther away. A pharmaceutical sales representative told me he was talking to an Arab medical student. The American representative backed away as the Arab was too close for him. The Arab student then abruptly turned and

walked away. He had been insulted because in his culture men stand close and to back off is an insult.

544. **Use gestures cautiously.** The meanings of gestures differ across cultures and when you are having difficulty with the language it is easy to use gestures. Be careful. The "okay" sign (the circle and three fingers raised), for example, means money in Japan, it's obscene in Brazil and means "worthless" in France.

545. **Know the cultural protocols around exchanging business cards.** In Japan the exchange of cards is part of the ritual greeting. You are to treat the card with respect. Look at the card. Do not just quickly put it in your pocket. In the United Arab Emirates exchange cards with the right hand only. The left hand is considered the dirty hand.

Plan for Differences in International Presentations

"I practiced starting my speech in French for weeks. I was going to begin by saying: 'Good morning, I am very pleased to be here and a thank you to my hosts.' I was so nervous that I initially froze, but I finally got it out and the audience was very pleased. It helped me break the ice and gave me confidence in handling the rest of the presentation."

546 **Adjust your speaking style.** Even if you are well-known and appreciated for a rapid-fire delivery in the United States, you will probably need to slow down and speak distinctly in order to be understood.

547. **Greet the audience in their language if you can.**

548. **Have notes.** It makes the presentation appear important since you took the time to prepare.

549. **Be cautious with starting with a joke.** The American sense of humor is not universal.

550. **Don't mock or criticize your competition.** This is usually considered rude.

551. **Include examples and references to your host country's culture.** Equally as important is using American references sparingly. When speaking to a Canadian group, I changed my American examples to Canadian ones. It was noted by the group and much appreciated.

552. **Have any speech or presentation you plan to give proofed in advance for possible culture-specific faux pas.** Find someone who knows the culture and speaks the language fluently to read your speech. If yours is a global organization you can often find someone within your own organization to help you. If not, check with your local language schools or universities.

Dress for International Success

"I was getting ready to give a presentation on international image to an international group in Paris. My French contact came up to me and said, 'Are you nervous?' I said, 'a little.' She was trying to make me feel better and said, 'Don't worry, when you get to the part about dressing for success, just tell them to buy Chanel! I thought about what she said, and before I flew home, stopped at the Chanel boutique and looked at their suits. She was right—the suits were gorgeous and wearing them has to make anyone feel good!"

553. **Don't assume you can wear the same clothing that you do while at home.** Even within the same company the guidelines may vary. You may have a business casual policy while your international divisions do not.

554. **If unsure, ask your host what is considered appropriate business attire.**

555. **Don't go native.** Dressing up in "native" clothing when on business is not appropriate—unless encouraged by your hosts.

556. **When in doubt, err on the safe side.** Wear good quality conservative clothing, generally a business suit.

When You're the Host

"I was entertaining one of my Arab colleagues at my home. I prepared chicken and added a little wine. Fortunately before I served the meal, I remembered the wine and that liquor is against his religion. I asked him if he wanted me to cook him a separate piece of chicken. He said yes. I was glad I asked."

557. **Be a gracious host.** It is a very gracious host who meets his or her visitors more than half way on etiquette issues. When visitors come to our country, they should be the ones adapting. Yet people don't always prepare or know our customs. It's also easy to forget or act out of habit before someone realizes it. A Brazilian colleague always kisses me on both cheeks when greeting me. And then he catches himself and extends his hand so we can shake hands. But I don't mind. I'm happy to do both.

558. **Know your visitor's greetings.** As just mentioned above, others may do their greeting. You will be less likely to be caught off guard if you are prepared.

559. **Learn about your visitor's culture.** Just as you prepare by reading and getting information before you go overseas for business, do the same prior to your guest's arrival. Find out as much as you can about your visitor's customs, attitudes and business values.

560. **Meet or send someone to meet the visitor at the airport.** How would you feel landing in an airport in a foreign country? It's a must for international visitors.

561. **Be aware of any food preferences or dietary restrictions.** If you will be taking the person to restaurants or having meals with him or her in your home, make sure you understand any food preferences or dietary restrictions— whether dictated by personal taste or religious beliefs. In addition to many guidebooks available, the person's secretary or assistant can provide you this kind of information. If you're not certain, ask the person directly.

562. **Have a basket of food or flowers sent to the visitor's room.** If you can find out the person's preferences or dietary restrictions beforehand, the gesture is made even more meaningful. Flowers have different meaning in different cultures so know what's appropriate before you send them (see section on gifts).

563. **Arrange for a driver and transportation during the visitor's stay.** Think about how you would feel getting around in a strange city.

564. **Plan interesting things for your visitor to do.** He or she will want to enjoy as much as possible of the local culture

during his or her stay. Provide materials about your city. Conduct a tour of your city if it is a first trip. If a visitor brings family members, if possible, arrange for some activities for them, also. This thoughtful gesture can help build good business relationships.

565. **Invite the visitor to your home.** Most international visitors enjoy the experience of seeing how Americans really live. When I coach Korean businessmen on learning American culture, they always look forward to the session that includes the "typical American dinner" at my house with my son.

Making Conversation the International Way

"I thought it would be difficult to talk to him. But once I realized how important soccer was to him, we started discussing the game and conversation just flowed."

566. **Talk on safe subjects.** General topics to avoid include controversial topics such as religion and politics. You also want to avoid the highly personal, such as your love life. You can certainly show an interest in another culture's politics or religion, just don't enter into a debate or offer criticism.

567. **Know about the country.** You must know about the country in order to have material to discuss. In addition to the items mentioned before, the following items will help you prepare for conversation: information about the main cities, the main industries, popular sports, special cultural activities, such as music and theater, and famous athletes, performers, artists or writers.

568. **Know how much small talk is appropriate.** The amount of small talk varies across cultures. In the United States, we usually get down to business usually after five to ten minutes of small talk, often even less. However, in other cultures, such as Mexico and Japan, small talk can literally go on for days. Remember that it's a part of establishing a business relationship.

569. **Be aware of differences in English.** You may be speaking with someone who speaks British English so be aware of vocabulary and language differences. For example, an "elevator" in the U.S. is called a "lift" in England. A "policeman" is a "bobby."

570. **Don't take for granted that the person speaking English will always understand you.** Rates of fluency vary when someone is speaking English as a second or even third language. Make sure you speak slower, not louder! You may want to follow up in writing to help ensure clarity.

571. **When you are speaking your language in a different country, do not assume that you will *not* be understood.** Your private conversation is not always private. Two Spanish men were speaking Spanish in a Parisian café and they assumed the woman next to them would not understand that they were discussing her! They knew she was an American as they had spoken to her, but they did not know that she spoke Spanish. She understood everything they had said and let them know that as she was leaving the café.

572. **Avoid jargon and buzzwords**—they don't translate well across languages. "We need to think outside the box" or "Let's hit the ground running" are not the kind of expressions that all will understand.

573. **Be cautious with humor.** Jokes and humor don't often translate well, either. Don't be humorous, but have a sense of humor—that's important when you're traveling.

574. **Ask questions and listen to the answers.** This will show that you are interested in learning about the culture and customs of the other person. Ask follow-up questions.

575. **Conversation at meals is not usually business in many cultures, such as France and China.** Unless your host initiates business talk during a meal, it's usually best not to bring up business topics.

576. **Learn a few key phrases in the language of the country you are visiting.** Saying hello, goodbye, good morning, please, thank you, etc. shows that you have an appreciation for the culture even if you don't speak the language. And the effort you exhibit by using them can pave the way for further conversation.

577. **Handle an interpreter correctly.** Though conversing through an interpreter may be more of a challenge, you still need to engage in small talk. Another challenge is that people often forget whom they're speaking with. Make sure you address the person you're speaking with and not the interpreter.

Dining Differences

"I was in Australia and was served kangaroo. I never had it before and was unsure about tasting it. I knew I was expected to try it so I did. I didn't like the taste but three bites didn't kill me. My hosts were so pleased. It was worth it!"

578. **Don't refuse what is offered to you.** Acceptance of food and drink is acceptance of the host. There really isn't any way to refuse food, unless you are allergic. Always try a little—even if it looks unappealing or is downright scary. The general guideline: Swallow quickly and don't ask!

579. **Wait until food is offered to you.** Helping yourself is an American custom.

580. **Be prepared for some unusual customs.** In many European restaurants dogs are allowed. In the Middle East I ate in a restaurant that had a sign that said "Women and Families." I couldn't go to the other side of the room—it was reserved for men only!

581. **Don't criticize or make negative comments about the food or restaurant.**

582. **Don't comment on table manners.** Good table manners in one country are not necessarily good manners in another. For example, making a slurping noise while eating is rude to Americans, but is accepted behavior to the Japanese.

583. **Watch your alcohol consumption.** I've said it before, but consuming too much alcohol during business dining or socializing is never a good idea no matter where you are and this includes when you're abroad. You need to be aware about the local customs around liquor, too. In many Middle Eastern countries, for example, it's against the religion, but in many European cultures you may be encouraged to drink up! Drinking wine can be an important part of their meal. If you do drink, just be smart about it.

584. **Adapt your eating schedule.** You are the visitor, so you must adapt to new mealtimes. In Latin America and

Spain, for example, the dinner hour is usually much later than the typical 6–7 P.M. North American standard.

585. **Don't bring your spouse along unless invited.** In some cultures, you should not expect to bring your spouse to business meals unless you are specifically invited to do so.

586. **Use utensils correctly.** In some cultures, you will be expected to eat with chopsticks or your fingers and you should follow the custom. In Europe you will see the continental use of the knife and fork (see Section 5 on socializing). In the Middle East I sat in a tent and ate food with my fingers. It was actually a lot of fun.

587. **Bring an appropriate gift.** If you're dining at someone's house, you should bring a hostess gift, but be careful. Check out the local customs before you bring any gift. (See section on gifts, page 160.)

International Writing Differences

"Why is he starting the letter Dear Rob. He doesn't know me well enough to do that!"
        —A German businessman speaking about a letter he received from an American account representative.

588. **Understand how cultural differences can influence writing.** Some cultures, including many in Asian, Middle Eastern, and Latin countries, are relationship-oriented. They want to have a relationship with you—often before they will do business with you. They may be very personal in their letters, telling you things

about their family or personal lives. Other cultures are more task-oriented. Relationships are emphasized less in these cultures, which include the United States, Canada, and Northern European countries. Writers tend to "get down to business" more quickly.

589. **Be sensitive to English as a second language (ESL) concerns.** As a business communications trainer and a former ESL instructor, I know that people can usually read English better than they can speak it. Yet, rates of fluency vary. Keep sentences short and your language simple. As you should when you speak, avoid the use of jargon, buzzwords, or regional expressions. Writing a sentence that states "We plan on a full court press" or "Let's go the whole nine yards on this project" may not be understood.

590. **Avoid humor and sarcasm.** As mentioned when speaking, if there's one thing that's not funny across cultures, it's humor. And it can be even harder to pull off successfully in writing. There are no non-verbal cues to help soften the words or convey your meaning.

591. **Use a formal salutation.** It's usually best to use last names when writing internationally. Americans have a tendency to go to first names very quickly. Don't use first names unless you are sure you can do so. Don't use nicknames, either.

592. **Don't cause date confusion.** 4/7/01 can be either April 7 or July 4, depending upon where your letter is heading. The solution is to spell out the date.

593. **Be aware of differences between American and British English.** Even if English is the first language of the recipient of your letter, you still must be aware of

differences in spelling and use of words and phrases. An American might write "I'll send you a bank check in two weeks" while a British person will write "I'll send you a bank cheque in a fortnight."

International Gift-Giving Guidelines

"I was going to give my Japanese colleagues coffee mugs with our company logo printed upon them as a gift. Until I turned them over and they said 'Made in China.' "

594. **Know your host's country's gift-giving customs.** There are lots of variables with regards to international gift giving. Read about the country or check with on-site mentors about a gift's appropriateness.

595. **Understand that gift giving is not necessarily optional or just a "nice" touch.** Some countries require business gifts; Japan does, others like Germany do not. Generally hostess gifts (when you go to someone's home for a meal or party) are appropriate in most countries. Know your company's policy with regards to giving and receiving gifts.

596. **Choose the right gift.** Ask yourself if the item violates any cultural or religious taboos. Sometimes an item can have a negative meaning. Avoid giving a clock in China. It's associated with funerals.

597. **When in doubt, choose a safe item.** It's hard to go wrong with nice pens, chocolates, pocket calculators, an atlas, and toys for children. Local crafts or illustrated books from your region of the country also make appropriate gifts.

598. **Always check the local customs before you bring or send flowers.** Flowers may have meanings that you don't know about. Certain flowers, such as white lilies in England, are for funerals only. Red roses are for lovers only in Germany. White flowers in Japan are associated with death.

599. **Be cautious with giving liquor as a gift.** In some countries imported liquor can be a good gift such as in Germany, Japan, Sweden. But alcohol is illegal in other countries like Saudi Arabia and Kuwait.

600. **Know the ritual around accepting a gift.** In some cultures, like South Korea and China, the gift will not be initially accepted. Be persistent. The refusal is part of the ritual.

601. **Know when to open or not open a gift.** In some cultures (Japan, China) it is bad form to open a gift when you receive it. By not opening it, you are showing that it is the giving of the gift that is important, not the actual item.

A FINAL NOTE

S O MANY LITTLE THINGS, so little time! Where should you start on your road to enhanced career success?

As I said in the beginning of this book, don't try to incorporate all 601 little things at once. You'll get frustrated. Start in an area where you know you need improvement. If you're not sure, just start at the beginning and work your way forward. Be open-minded. Don't dismiss a detail until you're sure it's not something you need to pay attention to.

Tune in. Think about changing your behavior for the better. Practice. Adjust. Move on.

Or, you can start with this list of twenty essentials. These are twenty things you can do right now to begin improving your career and working life. Though I can't guarantee that you'll get a big promotion next week, I can guarantee that if you become aware of and practice the little things below, your working life will improve. You will get along better with others. You will feel better about yourself. Other people will view you in a more professional light.

But you won't know until you give it a try. Good luck in your career journey and I'd love to hear your success story.

The Top 20 Little Things You Can Pay Attention To Right Now To Have A Better Work Day and Advance Your Career

1. **Greet and acknowledge others.** In my opinion, the number one detail that can eliminate conflict in the workplace is so simple—say "Hello," "Good morning," and "Have a nice day," etc. Make sure you shake hands too.

2. **Don't interrupt.** I hear this again and again—people don't like to be interrupted. Not only is this rude, it shows you're not listening but planning what you're going to say next.

3. **Wear appropriate clothing.** It's often one of the first things people will notice about you! What you wear can enhance your professional image or take away from it. You want it to work for you, not against you.

4. **Be aware of your facial expressions.** Many people have very stern facial expressions and don't even know it. You don't want people thinking you are upset with them.

5. **Speak loudly enough to be heard.** Many people speak too softly. If your volume is low, you can then become invisible and easy to ignore. People can speak and literally no one hears them.

6. **Use humor wisely.** Humor can be a lifesaver in embarrassing or stressful situations. But you can also bomb badly. You must use humor appropriately—especially in the workplace.

7. **Use polite language.** I know you know you're supposed to speak politely, but we don't always take the time to say such simple words as "please," "thank you," or "I appreciate your effort." Try it—it will make a huge difference in how people respond to you.

8. **Accept compliments.** Refusing a compliment is not gracious, it's silly and makes you look unprofessional.

9. **Understand the point of the business meal is not food.** You dine to conduct business and establish relationships. You may need to eat, but you are not there for the food.

10. **Stay sober.** Here's a general guideline that every one should memorize and practice: business and liquor don't mix! Drunk business people often behave unprofessionally, inappropriately and say and do things that come back to haunt them later.

11. **Continue learning and stay up to date with technology.** The world is changing and you don't want to be left behind. And yes, technology changes fast but the people who make an effort to keep up with it are the ones who make themselves valuable to their organizations.

12. **Exercise.** It's critical that you exercise regularly to control your stress and maintain health. Take advantage of company gyms and lunchtime aerobics. Even a brisk walk at lunch can do the trick.

13. **Have positive confrontations when appropriate.** Understand that you have the right to speak up and say something if another person's behavior is bothersome or annoying. It's so much better than pretending you don't care or complaining about the other person to your co-workers.

14. **When doing business internationally understand that you are the one who needs to adapt.** You are the visitor; you must be the one who changes his or her behav-

ior. The old adage, "When in Rome, do as the Romans do" is absolutely true.

15. **Understand that the quality of your business writing always counts.** And this includes e-mail. Don't make the mistake of thinking, "Oh this is just a quick note or fax, it's not like a formal letter…" If it's for business, the quality of your writing always matters and you will be judged for it.

16. **Don't e-mail when you're angry or upset.** It's too easy to send the message and you may regret it later. At the very least, give yourself a twenty-four-hour cooling off period and then decide if you still want to send the message.

17. **Don't answer your phone while you have a visitor in your office.** The participants of my seminars tell me this is really annoying behavior that they resent. If you're expecting an important call and someone stops in your office, let them know you're waiting for an important call. Otherwise, if you answer your phone while speaking with someone, you're in effect saying, "You're not as important as the person who might be calling."

18. **Do not use call waiting in business.**

19. **Be considerate when sharing space with others.** Don't let your cell phone ring when sharing space with others. Put it on vibrate. It's disturbing to others! If you are in a crowded area and receive a call, leave the room to talk.

20. **Always leave your name and number at the beginning and *at the end of a voice mail message*.** You can't assume that the person you're calling remembers your

phone number or is accessing their voice mail from his or her office. Plus, you save the person from looking it up and people appreciate this small courtesy.

ACKNOWLEDGMENTS

My sincere thanks and gratitude to my seminar participants and their employers, my clients. Their willingness to share their experiences helped me to develop this material. Thanks also to my editor, Matthew Lore. As always he was a pleasure to work with, and his guidance and assistance have been invaluable. I would also like to thank my agent Ellen Greene for her encouragement and my associate, Joyce Hoff, whose words of wisdom are always helpful. And last but never least, a special thanks to my son, Jacob.

ABOUT THE AUTHORS

BARBARA PACHTER is a business communications consultant, speaker, and seminar leader who speaks nationally and internationally on topics including assertiveness, business etiquette, international communications, women's issues, and presentation skills. She has conducted over 1,300 skill-building seminars for clients including NASA, Merck & Co., IBM, Arthur Anderson, and Pfizer, Inc. She is an adjunct professor at Rutgers University, author of *The Power of Positive Confrontation*, also published by Marlowe & Company, and the co-author of four books on business etiquette and communications skills, including *The Prentice Hall Complete Business Etiquette Handbook*. She lives in Cherry Hill, New Jersey.

SUSAN MAGEE is an award-winning writer whose articles and stories have appeared in many magazines and newspapers around the country. She lives in Conshohocken, Pennsylvania.

Barbara Pachter can be reached at:

Pachter & Associates
P.O. Box 3680
Cherry Hill, NJ 08034
Telephone (856) 751-6141
Fax (856) 751-6857
E-mail: pachter@ix.netcom.com
www.pachter.com